# 101

# Information
# Technology

# 101 KEY IDEAS

# Information Technology

**Stephen Gorard and Neil Selwyn**

TEACH YOURSELF BOOKS

For UK orders: please contact Bookpoint Ltd, 130 Milton Park, Abingdon, Oxon OX14 4SB. Telephone: (44) 01235 827720. Fax: (44) 01235 400454. Lines are open from 9.00–6.00, Monday to Saturday, with a 24-hour message answering service. Email address: orders@bookpoint.co.uk

For U.S.A. order enquiries: please contact McGraw-Hill Customer Services, P.O. Box 545, Blacklick, OH 43004-0545, U.S.A. Telephone: 1-800-722-4728. Fax: 1-614-755-5645.

For Canada order enquiries: please contact McGraw-Hill Ryerson Ld., 300 Water St, Whitby, Ontario L1N 9B6, Canada. Telephone: 905 430 5000. Fax: 905 430 5020.

Long renowned as the authoritative source for self-guided learning – with more than 30 million copies sold worldwide – the *Teach Yourself* series includes over 300 titles in the fields of languages, crafts, hobbies, business and education.

*British Library Cataloguing in Publication Data*
A catalogue record for this title is available from The British Library.

*Library of Congress Catalog Card Number:* On file

First published in UK 2001 by Hodder Headline Plc., 338 Euston Road, London, NW1 3BH.

First published in US 2001 by Contemporary Books, A Division of The McGraw-Hill Companies, 1 Prudential Plaza, 130 East Randolph Street, Chicago, Illinois 60601 U.S.A.

The 'Teach Yourself' name and logo are registered trade marks of Hodder & Stoughton Ltd.

Copyright © 2001 Stephen Gorard and Neil Selwyn

Cover illustration by Mike Stones
Typeset by Transet Limited, Coventry, England.
Printed in Great Britain for Hodder & Stoughton Educational, a division of Hodder Headline Plc, 338 Euston Road, London NW1 3BH by Cox & Wyman Ltd, Reading, Berkshire.

| Impression number | 10 9 8 7 6 5 4 3 2 |
| --- | --- |
| Year | 2007 2006 2005 2004 2003 2002 |

# Contents

Algorithm   1
Anthropomorphism   2
Apple   3
Arithmetic-logic unit   4
Artificial intelligence   5
ASCII   6
Babbage, Charles   7
Batch/real-time   8
Baud   9
Binary   10
Boolean logic   11
Central processing unit   12
Complement subtraction   13
Computer   14
Computer literacy   15
Computer mediated
    communication   16
Computerphobia   17
Corruption   18
Cyberfeminism   19
Cyberpunk   20
Cyberspace   21
Cyborg   22
Data   23
Data structure   24
Digital   25

Digital divide   26
E-   27
E-Commerce   28
Edutainment   29
E-mail   30
Engelbart, Douglas   31
Error propagation   32
Execution cycle   33
File access   34
File security   35
Floating point   36
Futurology   37
Fuzzy logic   38
Garbage in, garbage out   39
Global village   40
Hackers   41
Hardware   42
Hopper, Grace   43
Human Computer Interaction
    44
Hypertext   45
IBM   46
Information   47
Information and
    communications
    technology   48

Information society   49
Information superhighway
   50
Input device   51
Interactivity   52
Internet   53
Interrupt   54
Legislation   55
Linux   56
Logical error   57
Lovelace, Ada   58
Luddism   59
Memory   60
Memory address   61
Microsoft   62
Moore's Law   63
Multimedia   64
Multi-tasking   65
National information
   infrastructure   66
Network   67
Network society   68
On/off-line   69
Operating system   70
Optical fibre   71
Output device   72
Pervasive computing   73
Programming language   74
Robotics   75

Simulation   76
Sinclair, Clive   77
Software   78
Software engineering   79
Stack   80
Storage device   81
Super-Panopticon   82
Syntax   83
Systems analysis   84
Technological addiction   85
Technological determinism
   86
Technological fix   87
Technological utopianism   88
Technology   89
Teleworking   90
Time–space compression   91
Translation   92
Turing, Alan   93
Universal access   94
Verification and validation
   95
Virtual community   96
Virtual machine   97
Virtual reality   98
Virus   99
von Neumann, John   100
World wide web   101

# *Introduction*

**W**elcome to the **Teach Yourself 101 Key Ideas** series. We hope that you will find both this book and others in the series to be useful, interesting and informative. The purpose of the series is to provide an introduction to a wide range of subjects, in a way that is entertaining and easy to absorb.

Each book contains 101 short accounts of key ideas or terms which are regarded as central to that subject. The accounts are presented in alphabetical order for ease of reference. All of the books in the series are written in order to be meaningful whether or not you have previous knowledge of the subject. They will be useful to you whether you are a general reader, are on a pre-university course, or have just started at university.

We have designed the series to be a combination of a text book and a dictionary. We felt that many text books are too long for easy reference, while the entries in dictionaries are often too short to provide sufficient detail. The **Teach Yourself 101 Key Ideas** series gives the best of both worlds! Here are books that you do not have to read cover to cover, or in any set order. Dip into them when you need to know the meaning of a term, and you will find a short, but comprehensive account which will be of real help with those essays and assignments. The terms are described in a straightforward way with a careful selection of academic words thrown in for good measure!

So if you need a quick and inexpensive introduction to a subject, **Teach Yourself 101 Key Ideas** is for you. And incidentally, if you have any suggestions about this book or the series, do let us know. It would be great to hear from you.

Best wishes with your studies!

Paul Oliver
Series Editor

# Algorithm

An algorithm is a formal solution to a problem, expressed as a sequence of procedural steps and decisions. An algorithm can be expressed in a natural language like English or a programming language that is understood by computers. An algorithm is used as the basis of computer software; defining the logic for any new piece of computer programming. The solution to a problem is expressed as an algorithm, traditionally using flowcharts or pseudo-code. This sequence of steps is then converted into a code using the syntax rules of the programming language involved. In essence, therefore, an algorithm is the same thing as a computer program but imagined as pure logic rather than in a machine executable language. For example, if a section of program is required to look through a file for a record with a specified name then the algorithm might be:

● Open file
● Continue
● Read next record
● Until record name = specified name
● End.

Assuming that each of these steps can be translated into a form that the computer understands then this algorithm is valid. It is therefore important for the steps to be as precise as possible. However, the following version of the algorithm is invalid, since it will not find the specified name if it is the first record in the file. It therefore contains a 'logical error'.

● Open file
● Read first record
● Continue
● Read next record
● Until record name = specified name
● End.

A complete algorithm may be constructed from a series of many such procedures, and then tested for completeness by means of a dry run (using a pencil and paper for example). It is not generally possible to prove that an algorithm is correct, merely to show that it gives satisfactory results in a range of common and extreme conditions. The possibility for errors increases with the length of the algorithm, so one of the main aims for computer programmers is to produce 'elegant algorithms' that are simple, refined and use as few procedural steps as possible.

*see also...*

*Logical error; Programming language*

1

# Anthropomorphism

**D**eriving from the Greek words for man (*anthropos*) and form (*morphe*), anthropomorphism is the attribution of human ideas, feelings, shape and other characteristics to non-human entities (such as when we talk of a computer 'making a mistake'). The practice of anthropomorphism has a long history, especially with regard to religion. This can be seen in the long-standing portrayal of gods and goddesses in human form with human traits and characteristics. The traditional tendency for human beings to turn to anthropomorphism when dealing with the supernatural has been complemented by the trend of anthropomorphizing technology. Indeed, endowing technology with human characteristics is a common way for people to deal with information technology. Many IT users have, for example, found themselves blaming 'the computer' for doing something or pleading with a photocopier to work.

In the same way that some people name their car, ascribing anthropomorphic attributes to IT raises technology to the status of a social actor which people can deal with more easily. Anthropomorphism is a useful means of rationalizing the increasingly greater role that IT is playing in society. The complex processes through which IT functions are difficult for most non-expert users to conceptualize. Transforming a technology into the more comprehensible realm of a human being capable of human action is an easier way of visualizing the seemingly 'invisible' processes that it goes through.

Despite this intuitive aspect of anthropomorphism, it is ultimately a restrictive means of understanding IT and society. In particular, the anthropomorphism of IT often leads to an overly technologically determinist view of technology – where IT automatically 'does' things which humans have to acquiesce to. This deferral of power and agency to technology obscures the non-technological shaping forces behind IT. For example, blaming 'the computer' for incorrectly carrying out a task, ignores the possibility of human error on the part of the user, as well as the wider influence of the software programmer, computer manufacturers and others who were involved in the development, design and structuring of the system.

> *see also...*
>
> *Technological determinism*

# *Apple*

Despite being a multi-national corporation, the Apple Computer Company continues to be seen by many computer users as embodying the libertarian ideals of early home computing. Apple computers are seen by their devotees as intuitive to use, stylish in design and creative in output. Above all, Apple computers are perceived to be person-orientated and to embody a 'human' side of computing. This distinction of Apple as the computer company of choice for the IT 'intelligentsia' is an interesting example of the social shaping of technology by commercial firms.

In part, this popular perception of Apple stems from the company's origins in the 'counter-culture' of the computer hobbyist movement of the 1970s and, in particular, the garages of two teenagers Steve Jobs and Steve Wozniak. The pair had been involved in the 'Homebrew' computer enthusiast club in Berkeley, California during the 1970s and decided in 1976 to form a company to sell Wozniak's Apple I computer. The Apple I and the subsequent Apple II and III models were among the first mass-produced personal computers in the US. With their plastic cases and colour graphics, these computers quickly established Apple as one of the first successes of the new pioneering domestic IT industry.

Apple's defining moment came with the development of their Macintosh computer. Borrowing heavily from features developed by Xerox research laboratories, the 'Mac' was based around a graphical user interface – allowing users to control the computer using a pointing device within the 'real-world' metaphor of a desktop. At a time when personal computers were still based around text-based displays and the typing in of complicated instructions via a keyboard, the Mac's far more user-friendly interface was a revelation. Apple reinforced this by marketing the Mac as a 'machine for the people'. Yet the attractiveness of the machine was hampered by some technical limitations until the development of a desktop publishing program and laser printer for the Mac brought about a renewed popularity amongst more 'artistic' computer users, especially designers and musicians. Subsequent Apple products have often been creatively designed and ingeniously marketed but have not always led to widespread commercial success.

> ## see also...
> *Hardware; IBM*

3

# Arithmetic-logic unit

The arithmetic-logic unit (ALU) is part of a computer system which contains the circuits and special memory locations where arithmetic and logical operations are performed. In its simplest form an ALU consists of an accumulator, a shift register, and an adder circuit.

The accumulator is a register that stores the results of any arithmetic or logical operation. It also usually provides an implied operand (see Memory address, p.61). A machine instruction such as 'Add immediate 57' might require the ALU to add the number 57 to the existing contents of the accumulator and store the result back in the accumulator.

A shift register is able to move the digits in any number to the left or right. In binary this has the effect of multiplying or dividing the number by two. In the same way that shifting a base 10 number to the left has the effect of multiplying by ten (so that 3070 is 10 times 307), so in base two 0110 is twice as much as 0011. This is a simple way for a computer to multiply or divide. To divide by eight, the number is moved to the shift register and shifted three places to the right (0101000 or 40 in base ten becomes 00000101 or five). To multiply by ten the binary number is shifted three places to the left (to multiply by eight), the original number is then shifted one place to the left (to multiply by two), and the two results are added together and the final answer placed in the accumulator. In this way, most arithmetic operations can be completed as a sequence of shifts and addition.

The adder circuit is also relatively simple since there are only four binary sums that can take place. If a sum is broken down into the separate digit pairs in each number, then the adder only needs to know that:

0+0=0
0+1=1
1+0=1 and
1+1=0 with a carry of 1 to
the next left digit.

More simply, the sum of two digits is 0 if the digits are the same, and 1 otherwise, and the carry is 0 unless both digits are 1. In terms of Boolean logic,
● the carry from the sum of two numbers such as A, B is: C=A AND B.
● the sum of A, B is: S=(A OR B) AND NOT C.

*see also...*

**Binary; Boolean logic; Complement subtraction; Memory address**

# Artificial intelligence

Artificial intelligence (AI) represents a branch of science concerned with the creation of machines that can 'think'. Despite considerable research in the area, the nature and aims of artificial intelligence remain contested – especially with regards to the exact definition of 'intelligence'. Conventional definitions of AI are often based around the 'Turing Test' which reasons that a machine can be considered intelligent if a human can not identify it as being a machine as opposed to a human.

AI can be represented on two levels. 'Strong' AI continues to pursue the belief that computers can be made to think at a level equal to, or more advanced than, humans. 'Weak' AI, on the other hand, concentrates on adding 'thinking-like' features to computers to make them more useful tools. Examples of 'weak' AI are numerous. Expert systems, for example, where a computer is programmed to make decisions in real-life situations are now used in areas such as medicine. Robotics applications have been developed where computers are programmed to see, hear and react to sensory stimuli. Perhaps the most publicized advances in AI have occurred in the area of games playing, most notably in 1997 when the super-computer 'Deep Blue' defeated the chess Grandmaster Gary Kasparov.

The key question remains whether 'strong' AI will ever be achievable. Although AI systems have been developed to perform an impressive range of tasks, the extent to which machines are truly 'thinking' for themselves is limited. Indeed, the majority of robotic applications are programmed to carry out complex yet repetitive tasks. Similarly, games playing programs follow a complex series of pre-programmed rules – they do not necessarily understand what they are doing. So far, machines have been made to behave and think like humans in areas based on 'formal' knowledge that can easily be transferred to symbolic form and encoded into machines. However, other forms of human action are based upon more 'tacit' forms of knowledge that is learnt in social situations and cannot be easily 'transferred'. Thus, unless computers can be programmed to become social actors only 'weak' AI is likely to be achievable.

*see also...*

*Robotics; Turing, Alan*

# ASCII

The American Standard Code for Information Interchange (ASCII) is a coding system that has become an industry-standard for representing textual data in binary form. Each character (such as the letter 'T') or function (such as the 'RETURN' button) on the keyboard is represented in memory by a unique sequence of eight binary digits (or bits). For example, the letter 'A' is stored in digital form as 11000000, 'B' is 01000001, and so on.

The notion of each character being represented by eight bits is such an important one that the unit of information has a special name – a byte. Any data or instructions entered into a computer are generally stored in this text (or 'source') form at first. Program instructions are then converted into actual instruction codes, so that the instruction 'Store' might be held in memory as five characters using five bytes of storage, but would be converted by translation into a function code taking only one or two bytes. Similarly, the base 10 number 1,024 might be entered into memory as a sequence of four bytes representing the ASCII codes for 1, 0, 2 and 4 respectively, before being converted to a binary value (i.e. 10000000000 in fixed-point format).

It is possible to represent the different patterns of 256 (or $2^8$) with eight binary digits. However ASCII only has agreed meanings for half (128) of these. Thus, any ASCII character could actually be represented by seven bits. So the code for 'A' is 65 (in base 10) or 1000000 (in binary), the <Carriage Return> is 13 (in base 10) or 0001101, and the full stop '.' is 42 (in base 10) or 0101010. The eighth digit is redundant and most commonly used as a parity bit. This means that the eighth bit (actually the first in the sequence) is set to 1 or 0 in order to make the total number of bits set to 1 an even number. This parity bit is set to 1 for the letter 'A' which otherwise has only one bit set (11000000), but not for 'B' which has two bits set already (01000001).

Parity acts as a useful protection against corruption, or unwanted alteration of data. If any character does not have an even number of bits set this means that at least one bit has been corrupted. Failing an internal parity check means that invalid data will not be used in further processing, since it is common that when one bit is corrupted it is a symptom of a wider problem.

*see also...*

*Binary; Information*

# Babbage, Charles

The British mathematician, economist, intellectual, and inventor, Charles Babbage (1792–1871), can now rightfully be seen as a founding architect of computing. His designs for a steam-driven brass mechanical computer were conceptually far ahead of their time and provided many of the principles that underpin modern-day computing.

Despite his many other interests and accomplishments, Babbage's lasting legacy was undoubtedly his work designing mechanical calculating machines. The first of these were his designs for a table-making machine known as the Difference Engine. Consisting of eighteen wheels and three axles, the Difference Engine created tables of values by calculating the common difference between terms in the sequence. Although it had no memory, it was envisaged that the Difference Engine could be used to print out tables of values – such as astronomical tables. However, before Baggage had completed the Difference Engine he switched his attention to a far more sophisticated machine, known as the Analytical Engine. The steam-driven Analytical Engine was designed to carry out any mathematical calculation, dictated by a series of instructions on loops of punched cards.

Amongst other innovative features the Analytical Engine had a memory capable of storing a thousand fifty-digit numbers and could perform calculations rapidly, based on previous instructions.

Both the Difference Engine and Analytical Engine were feats of engineering, but neither were actually constructed in Babbage's lifetime due to their sheer scale. Nevertheless, the ambitious and complex design of Babbage's computational machines were part of the development of the wider field of computing. Indeed, despite the theoretical nature of much of Babbage's work, the robustness of his ideas was only fully recognized over a century later with the development of the first electronic computers. Babbage's notion of punch cards storing instructions proved to be a forerunner of computer programming and input devices, with the Analytical Engine also utilizing a random-access memory in the form of a rack of columns. In 1991 a group of British engineers constructed a Difference Engine following Babbage's plans. The machine worked perfectly and could calculate numbers up to 31 digits long.

## see also...

*Computer; Lovelace, Ada*

# Batch/real-time

Most users' experience of using a computer will have been in real-time. This means that the computer is operating at the same time as the user. So, if you ask the computer to perform a task it is conducted immediately. You can open a file and read data from it, then use that data in another process straight away, within the limitations of speed imposed by the processor and peripherals. Where a computer system or network is being used by more than one person at once the appearance of real-time use is created by alternating control of the system between users (and is noticeable only when so many users are involved that the response seems 'sluggish'). Computers operate at colossal speeds in comparison to human operations like typing or mechanical operations like printing. All users appear to be on-line simultaneously (although, of course, one processor can only be doing one thing at a time).

An alternative way of using a computer is in batch-processing mode, which is more common in commercial applications with larger computer systems and many users. Here the operating system assembles all programs and tasks into batches and executes them in an efficient priority order, and many activities are conducted off-line.

Real-time can be clearly more convenient for an individual user, and some activities can only be executed in real-time. Interactive processes, such as order-entry, on-line banking, flight simulators and arcade games, would not make sense in batch mode. Batch has two advantages however. It does not require the user to be present while the computer does its job, such as calculating the monthly payroll for a large firm. In this way, the computer can sometimes replace the need for a human operator rather than simply assist a user in carrying out lengthy or complex tasks. Batch processing also makes more efficient use of processor and peripheral time and is therefore more cost-effective. Most machines are idle even when being used. As I am typing this sentence at a brisk 30 characters per minute, the computer that I am the sole user of is being 'starved' of input for much of that minute. It could be running a lengthy statistical analysis of a huge dataset at the same time (as a batch process) and still have the capacity for more.

see also...

*Multi-tasking; On/off-line*

# Baud

**N**amed after the telegraphic pioneer Jean Baudot (1845–1903), a Baud is a unit measuring the speed of information transmission in any communication system. Traditionally, a Baud represents a transfer rate of approximately one binary digit per second, although this value may vary depending upon the precise nature of the system. In practice, the speed of information transfer through any channel also depends on the quality of transmission, and on whether the transfer is serial or parallel. Where the channel is open to interference, the quality of the transmission is likely to be lower and the speed has to be less to compensate. This is why a modem often has a choice of Baud rates to operate at. This quality/speed compromise is similar to that between fidelity and band width in radio transmission. A serial transfer means that the channel is only one bit 'wide'. The more common parallel transfer means, in effect, that several channels are operating simultaneously, each delivering the same number of bits per second. Typically, there might be eight 'wires' in parallel carrying all of the bits in one ASCII character at the same time. In this case the Baud rate would be an estimate of the number of characters transmitted per second.

An important factor to take into consideration with the speed of information transmission is 'noise'. Noise is the term used by engineers to denote background fluctuations and interference in a system. Noise tends to corrupt messages between the various components of an information system, meaning that the bits received at one end are different from those sent from the source. Of course, in terms of one binary digit any corruption is total, since there are only two states. A corrupted bit contains the exact opposite to what was intended (0 becomes 1 or 1 becomes 0). This one bit change might have the effect of turning a letter 'A' into a letter 'B' or the number 65 into the number 193. Therefore, communications systems generally incorporate a safety check, similar to the idea of verification and validation. The simplest kind of check on the accuracy of a message is consistency. The message can be sent twice and the two received versions compared. If corruption is caused by random variation then this will show up as a difference between the two versions. Further precaution against corruption include the use of parirty checks, check digits and hash sums.

> ## see also...
> ### ASCII; Verification and validation

# Binary

The binary numbering system is fundamental to the logic of a digital computer. All information is coded in one of two mutually exclusive states such as the presence or absence of an electronic signal, the presence or absence of a magnetic field, the clockwise or anti-clockwise direction of a magnetic field, or a light or dark stripe. For convenience these two states are expressed using the digits 0 or 1. Each such digit is termed a 'bit', short for binary digit, and represents the smallest amount of information possible in any system. A bit is therefore enough information to decide between two alternatives, such as yes/no or stop/go.

By combining bits into sequences it is possible to represent more complex information. A group of two bits has four distinct combinations or patterns:

00, 01, 10, 11

A group of three bits has eight distinct combinations, four bits have 16 combinations and so on. In fact any group of n bits has $2^n$ combinations. In a computer there is usually a standard group size, called the 'word' length. Although a bit is the basic unit of information, it is too small for most practical purposes. Therefore, each computer has a word length representing the smallest amount of information it usually handles at once. Note that this length is usually a power of two, such as 16 or 64. In a machine with a 64 bit word length, each memory location would be able to store 64 bits, the data and address buses would usually handle 64 bits, each special register (such as the accumulator) would have 64 bits, and each machine code instruction would have 64 bits (the machine would therefore be able to distinguish between $2^{64}$ or 18 million million million different instructions).

Any 'word' could represent a variety of different types of information. If the patterns are treated as an integer then they follow the rules for binary. The right-most digit represents units of one, the next represents units of two, the next units of four and so on. For example, the binary number 00101010 is equivalent to the base ten number '42', or zero ones, one two, zero fours, one eight, zero sixteens, and one thirty-two.

| 128 | 64 | 32 | 16 | 8 | 4 | 2 | 1 |
|-----|----|----|----|---|---|---|---|
| 0 | 0 | 1 | 0 | 1 | 0 | 1 | 0 |

**see also...**

*Digital; Floating point*

# Boolean logic

This is a form of arithmetic-logic devised by, and named after, George Boole, a nineteenth-

If X, Y, are the input signals, then the output from an AND gate is only 1 when both X and Y are 1, for example. The

| X | Y | X AND Y | X OR Y | X NAND Y | X NOR Y |
|---|---|---------|--------|----------|---------|
| 0 | 0 | 0 | 0 | 1 | 1 |
| 0 | 1 | 0 | 1 | 1 | 0 |
| 1 | 0 | 0 | 1 | 1 | 0 |
| 1 | 1 | 1 | 1 | 0 | 0 |

century British mathematician whose work has been of fundamental importance to the design of computers. Boolean logic works using the binary opposition 'True' or 'False', and is therefore suitable for working with a binary numbering system (using 1 and 0 to denote true and false). Logic circuits are built using logic gates (equivalent to the basic electronic components of a computer), and banks of these logic circuits are used to build to the component parts of computer systems.

Boolean logic contains five main operators, several of which can be combined to form others (see table). The first operator is NOT, which simply reverses the signal or truth-value, making 1 into 0 and 0 into 1. The other four operators – AND, OR, NAND, NOR – all use two operands. Their effect on two signals, labelled X and Y, is summarized in the table.

order of X, Y, is not important for any gates, so that the row starting 0 1 has the same outcome from each gate as the row starting 1 0. It is also clear that NAND is simply the inverse (NOT) of AND, while NOR is the inverse of OR. In addition X NAND Y is the same as NOT(X OR Y), while X NOR Y is the same NOT(X AND Y) – these equivalencies are known as the laws of Augustus De Morgan (a mathematician, 1806–1871). These relationships mean that any logic circuit can be built using only one type of gate, such as NAND gates. This, in turn, means that computer processors can be built from pre-printed circuit boards containing only one component. The advantages of this in terms of cost and miniaturization are considerable.

*see also...*

*Arithmetic-logic unit; Binary*

# Central processing unit

**W**ithin a computing machine the central processing unit is the actual computer, as distinct from the more visible peripherals. The central processing unit (or CPU) has three major components – the control circuits, the arithmetic-logic unit, and the main memory (the last two of these are discussed in more detail elsewhere). In combination these components form the basis for the standard model of the computer as expressed in the von Neumann machine. The term 'microprocessor' usually refers to a CPU on one microchip – or at least the control and arithmetic units on one chip. Connected to these three components are the peripheral devices permitting communication with the outside world (such as the keyboard) and for long-term storage (such as the disc drive).

As soon as the computer is switched on, the CPU begins to execute instructions according to a fixed cycle. At the heart of the CPU is a 'clock' which pulses regularly. On each pulse, the instructions are fetched in sequence from the memory and each is converted to a micro-program of actions. These actions generally consist of two types of events. Data, in the form of 'words', is moved from one place to another via central bundles of electronic pathways called 'buses'. Control signals, in the form of bits, are sent from the control unit to the relevant parts of the CPU.

A simple example of how this works follows. If the current instruction involves copying a number in the instruction register (the operand) to the accumulator, a control (on/off) signal is set to the instruction register which releases the operand to the data bus. The data bus is connected to all CPU registers and to the main memory, and therefore delivers the operand to all of these automatically. However, none of these other registers allows the new data to overwrite their contents. At the entrance to each register is an AND logic gate. Changing the contents of any register requires two things – the data *and* the control signal. In the example, only the accumulator is affected. Similar actions produce all CPU effects, and the micro-program for any machine instructions involves a sequence of these control signals. Each part of the CPU has a specific function. The instruction does not therefore need to tell each part *what* to do (the adder can only add and so on), only *when* to do it.

## see also...

*Arithmetic-logic unit; Execution cycle; Memory*

# *Complement subtraction*

In the early days of calculators, several complex technical problems arose from the concept of 'borrowing' during subtraction. It is easier when designing a machine to remodel the process of subtraction itself. One solution is called 'nine's complement subtraction'. In this the number to be subtracted is subtracted from a number consisting of all nines. The result is added to the number to be subtracted from, one is added to the result of that, and the carry at the left hand end is ignored. This may sound even more confusing than normal subtraction with borrowing, but does have the major advantage that no borrowing is ever required.

To calculate $3409 - 1874$ usually involves two borrows: $9 - 4$ is 5, $0 - 7$ won't go so borrow 10, $10 - 7$ is 3, $3 - 8$ won't go, so borrow 10, $13 - 8$ is 5, $2 - 1$ is 1. The answer, reading backwards, is 1535. But using nine's complement the process goes as follows.

$$9999 - 1874 = 8125$$
$$3409 + 8125 = 11534$$

Ignore the carry to the fifth digit, and add 1, gives 1535. What is happening is that 9999 is being added to the sum to avoid borrowing, then 10000 is being subtracted and 1 added at the end to cancel out the 9999.

A very similar process takes place in binary subtraction where it is called one's complement. To subtract one binary number from another, the one's complement of the first is added to the second, any carry off the left hand end is ignored and one is added to the answer. The base 10 subtraction of $23 - 9$ would be $10111 - 01001$ in binary.

$$11111 - 01001 = 10110$$
$$10111 + 10110 = 101101$$

Ignore the carry to the fifth digit and add 1, gives 01110 (or 14 in base 10). However, in binary this process has another key advantage in addition to never requiring borrowing. The one's complement of a number is always simply the inverse of its digits (where 0 becomes 1 and 1 becomes 0). This is equivalent to the logical operation NOT. To subtract B from A in binary, we can add NOT B to A, add 1 and ignore the carry. Therefore, in binary, a subtraction can be done by addition only. The practical advantage of this in terms of computer design is that the only arithmetic circuit necessary in a computer is an adder.

*see also...*

**Binary; Boolean logic**

# Computer

Synonymous for many people with information technology, a computer is simply a programmable machine that can manipulate symbols. The defining characteristics of computers are that they can be programmed to perform many different functions and can both store and retrieve large amounts of data. In this way, computers can carry out very complex procedures rapidly, reliably, precisely and repeatedly, without fatigue. In order to do this, a computer relies on four main components: *memory* (and storage devices) to allow it to store programs and data; a *central processing unit* to execute programs; *input* devices which allow the user to enter data and instructions; *output* devices through which the results can be seen by the user. Despite the fact that modern-day computers can run 3-D arcade games and handle powerful business applications, they are still fundamentally based around the actions of the earliest computing machines, i.e. processing and manipulating numbers.

The early computers were large 'mainframe' machines in academic, research and military settings – often occupying entire rooms and taking hours 'if not days' to perform tasks. Since the 1950s, developments in electronic technology have allowed computers to become smaller, faster and more powerful. The major technical breakthrough was the use of transistors, rather than the unreliable valves, as relays. The transformation of the computer from a powerful, specialist tool to a hugely popular artefact came about with the development of the personal computer – small single-user computers capable of running software. Now, unlike earlier 'stand-alone' versions, modern-day personal computers are networkable, thus extending their capabilities by their ability to communicate with other computers.

The effects of computers on society have been profound. Such is the range of applications that computers can carry out that they are more than just an efficient information processing tool and have opened up new ways of dealing with information. Many people would argue that the computer has fundamentally changed the way that we see and understand the world – offering us the opportunity to experience things that would not have been possible before.

## see also...

Central processing unit; Program

14

# Computer literacy

ince computers were first made widely available at the end of the 1970s, it has been argued that one of the main aims of education and work should be to equip people with the expertise and familiarity needed in order to use computers – commonly referred to as computer literacy. Yet after 20 years of use, computer literacy remains an ambiguous and ill-defined concept. On the one hand the term alludes to a layperson's knowledge and understanding of a specialized field, whilst on the other it can suggest quite exact skills and competencies. Some people see computer literacy as the acquisition of specific software skills, word processing in particular. However, other authors suggest broader definitions, for example, that computer literacy can be considered to mean possessing the understanding and skills necessary to live in a computerized society. Arthur Luehrmann (1981) is even less specific, offering that 'computer literacy is the ability to *do* computing'.

Although it can be argued that these latter definitions are justified in avoiding the assumption that skills alone constitute complete 'literacy', they are phrased in such a general manner as to make them of little practical use. This is a problem in attempting to define practically the concepts behind the phrase 'computer literacy'. Many people have tended to take a narrow 'functional' approach to 'computer literacy' solely in terms of specific skills gained. Like numeracy and literacy skills (on which the metaphor is based) computer literacy is most noticeable in comments about its absence – the so-called skills gap. However, since the mid-1980s there has also been a call to expand these definitions into a broader category of 'technical literacy', thus recognizing the need for people to understand the social and cultural functions of the computer alongside the traditional 'expertise literacy' already discussed. As it stands, computer literacy is a vague term often used without an exact definition of what is meant beyond stressing the importance of computers in society. The metaphor is also inappropriate since, unlike traditional literacy that can be mastered in youth and preserved throughout adult life, the requirements for computer literacy change rapidly with technological progress.

*see also...*

Computerphobia

# Computer mediated communication

In its widest sense, computer mediated communication (CMC) describes any form of communication which takes place via computers. However, with the rise of the Internet, the term popularly refers to interpersonal communication facilitated through computer networks. In this way, CMC is often contrasted with conventional 'face-to-face' communication where people interact with each other in the same place at the same time. Computer mediated communication is significantly different from face-to-face communication in that participants generally only see what is on the computer screen. Therefore, they rely primarily on what has been written, rather than the non-verbal forms of communication that form a large part of face-to-face interaction (although video-conferencing is growing in frequency and practicality). Computer mediated communication can either be synchronous (where communication takes place in 'real-time') or asynchronous (where communication is fragmented and takes place over time). Popular examples of CMC include Internet chat and bulletin boards, e-mail, newsgroups and even mobile-phone based text messaging.

The significance of computer mediated communication lies in its distinctiveness from other forms of communication. As a hybrid form of oral and written language, much attention has been paid to how CMC may be leading to changing forms of language. Although many instances of CMC do resemble written forms of speech, it often relies on a simplified register. For example, CMC can be loose in terms of conventional punctuation and spelling – often relying heavily on acronyms and abbreviations. An interesting example of how CMC is leading to new forms of discourse is the use of 'emoticons' – textual representation of feelings – to overcome the lack of non-verbal communication. The evolving use of symbols such as :-) to denote a joke or sarcasm represent the integration of effective characteristics of speech into a text format.

As well as the ways that people interact with each other, CMC is often argued to be a more democratic means of communication, as the lack of visual identifiers when interacting give participants more equality of opportunities to speak. In this way, traditional barriers to communication such as shyness or lack of social status are less of a problem.

## see also...

E-mail; Virtual community

# Computerphobia

Although exact definitions vary, the phenomenon of 'computerphobia' can be seen as the fear and apprehension felt by an individual when considering the implications of using IT, even when the technology poses no real or immediate threat. In other words, computerphobia clouds an individual's perception of the computer, making it appear somehow 'not for them'. This can have a serious effect on people's performance when using IT, or indeed whether they choose to come into contact with new technologies at all.

Early studies in the 1980s estimated that 30–35 per cent of all users experienced some degree of anxiety when they first used a computer. At the time, some people argued that computerphobia differed little from the anxieties which have surrounded the introduction of other technologies throughout history – and that anxieties about using IT would inevitably diminish as computers became more commonplace. Yet, two decades on, research suggests that computerphobia remains just as relevant.

Suggested reasons for computerphobia consist of three types: psychological, sociological and operational. Psychological factors can include the perception of computers as something that users have little or no control over.

Other psychological factors are linked to the feeling that using a computer can be a threat to some users' self-esteem, confidence or self-efficacy. Sociological factors leading to computerphobia include the negative stereotyping by individuals of other computer users (i.e. 'nerds') and the lack of social interaction associated with using a computer. Finally, operational factors refer to anxieties surrounding actually operating and interacting with the machine. This can relate either to hardware interaction (using a mouse, switching a computer on and off) or interacting with various software packages. The inability to perform routine operations that others seemingly find effortless can therefore lead people to avoid using computers.

Although still seen to be a major factor behind people's avoidance of using IT in contemporary society, there is a danger in wholly 'blaming' the individual for not using technology. Although useful, the concept of computerphobia overlooks many of the wider factors underlying individuals' non-use of technology as well as stigmatizing people who decide not to engage with IT as irrational phobics.

see also...
Luddism

17

# Corruption

Corruption refers to any unwanted alteration of data. This can often happen during transcription of information for data entry to a computer, when a column of figures is copied incorrectly by the operator. Corruption can also occur during transmission of data between computers, or between a computer and a peripheral, when background 'noise' on a telephone line scrambles the ASCII code for a piece of text. It can happen during storage of data on a file system when a magnetic storage device suffers loss of accuracy through deterioration of the magnetic surface (known as dropout). In each of these examples, the data becomes corrupted (or loses integrity). This means that any future operations involving such data will produce erroneous results (garbage in, garbage out). Any computer system given poor quality information to work with will produce poor quality results. This is the significance of data corruption.

As corrupt data will be of little use and can even lead to dangerous results, most systems are designed to detect the presence of corruption. Defence against corruption occurs in two distinct phases. First: simply detecting that corruption has taken place is important so that the affected data is not used. Second: it is useful to be able to correct the errors in corrupted data. A whole range of defences are used routinely, and often automatically, in computer systems, to prevent, detect and correct bad data. In general, these defences are referred to as 'verification and validation'. The techniques involved include check digits, hashing, parity, range checks, labelling, write-permit tabs, generations of files, and backup file copies. Several of these are dealt with elsewhere in this book.

The generation of files (or 'grandfather/father/son') method is a simple and effortless way of providing some security for your files. Originally developed for use in batch mode file updating, it is still useful in the more common real-time operations today. If you were writing an essay on a word processor and storing it on a floppy disc then the method would work as follows. Each time you open the file in order to continue writing or editing you immediately save it as another file (the next generation), on another disc. You can then rotate two discs, so that if one copy becomes corrupted you have at least the next most recent copy. While not perfect the method requires no extra effort, unlike copying files.

## see also...

*ASCII; Verification and validation*

# Cyberfeminism

For many feminists, IT is just another aspect of the social world which is fundamentally organized by gender and dominated by men and boys. Against this male-dominated background, a range of feminist responses to information technology has emerged since the 1970s. A 'liberal feminist' perspective, for example, would argue that IT is an opportunity for women to 'catch up' with men. Conversely, an 'eco-feminist' perspective would argue that IT is yet another male attempt to control women and nature via technology. This school of feminism would therefore urge women to 'reject' IT as a masculine oppressive technology and seek to develop new and alternative technologies.

However, over the last ten years a new wave of feminist thinkers has begun to reject these established viewpoints. The 'beat them at their own game' stance of the liberal feminists is seen to restrict women and technology to conforming to male modes of IT use, whereas eco-feminism is seen as unhelpful in its outright rejection of new technologies. An emerging group of 'cyberfeminist' thinkers take the alternate view that instead of being something to either acquiesce to or reject, IT is something that women can challenge, change and ultimately control for themselves.

In particular, cyberfeminists are interested in the potential for IT to allow women to control and (re)construct their bodies, identities and political positions. For example, cyberspace is seen as a place where gender becomes fluid, thus providing an environment where women can actively challenge and overturn traditional forms of gender socialization. Cyberfeminist thinking tends to concentrate on emerging virtual reality and cyborg technologies. In practice, cyberfeminist activity has largely taken the form of Internet based activity – such as the 'cyber-girl' on-line groups and publications.

Cyberfeminism, then, can be seen as a provocative reconceptualization of gender and technology. As such, its stance can be criticized for being overtly utopian in its often positive portrayal of IT. However, cyberfeminist theory provides a powerful alternative to the usual male-orientated viewpoints of technology and society.

> **see also...**
> *Cyberpunk*

# Cyberpunk

**C**yberpunk is a term originally emanating from a new wave of science fiction writing which emerged during the 1980s, painting a dark and often pessimistic picture of technological society in the near future. Through authors such as William Gibson and Bruce Sterling, as well as films such as *Blade Runner*, *Terminator* and *Alien*, the cyberpunk body of literature described societies dominated by oppressive systems or political regimes founded on information technologies such as computer networks, artificial intelligence, cybernetics and virtual reality. Crucially, such work focused on marginalized people living 'on the edge' of society and their efforts to use these technologies to survive and fight back against the system.

Cyberpunk was quickly seized upon by groups of computer users as a term of self-reference – with many people seeing similarities between cyberpunk fiction and their own experiences of the emerging 'technosystem' in the real world. So cyberpunk also came to refer to a real-life subculture – including so-called 'hackers' and 'crackers' (very able programmers who try to break into other computer systems), as well as other computer users concerned with using IT for their own purposes, often against companies and other 'official' bodies.

Cyberpunk should be seen as a key idea in information technology due to the issues it raises about technology and the near future. Some cyberpunk concepts, such as cyberspace, have already had profound effects on the way that we see technology. Its wider emphasis on the marginalization of groups in technological societies also has resonance with current debates over the 'digital divide' (wherein sections of society are progressively excluded by their inability to own or use technology). Yet it is the pessimistic view of a society where technology is used oppressively by the state and corporations to dominate a majority of citizens which raises the most interesting questions about technology and society. In this way, cyberpunk presents a reverse picture to the utopian view of an information society where technology has only beneficial applications and empowers individuals. As with all attempts at describing the future, cyberpunk tends towards an extreme and ultimately fictionalized vision of technology and society.

## see also...

*Cyberspace; Hackers*

# Cyberspace

The term 'cyberspace', first used by the novelist William Gibson in the 1982 short story *Burning Chrome*, has risen to prominence as technologies such as the Internet continue to grow in popularity. In Gibson's novels, cyberspace was a fictional 'world in the wires' known as the 'matrix' connecting all of the world's computers and information systems. Now cyberspace is broadly taken to refer to the non-physical 'spaces' created by computer systems, where people can interact with each other and experience computer-simulated worlds. In this way, cyberspace refers to an abstract notion of a computer-mediated place which users can manipulate and move through by issuing commands to computers and other virtual reality technologies.

It is the notion of cyberspace as non-physical 'space' that makes it so contentious. For many people cyberspace is an exciting and fundamentally *new* place for interaction and exploration. It symbolizes the potential for technologies to improve existing ways of work and leisure and is often portrayed as a 'new world' waiting to be explored and used beneficially. Thus, many people see cyberspace as an alternative terrain, where better forms of democracy, politics, ethics and even personal identities can be created. Yet others would argue that this idealized view ignores the fact that cyberspace is not a self-contained alternative to the existing world, but inherently part of it. For example, cyberspace is dependent on the economic realities of the world, as can be seen in the ongoing commercialization of the world wide web. Cyberspace is an extension of, rather than a replacement for, the real world.

It is therefore important to exercise a degree of restraint when discussing the idea of cyberspace and treat it as William Gibson originally intended; as a 'consensual hallucination'. Cyberspace is a place that does not exist – a fantasy rather than a reality. At best, it is a metaphor through which we can conceptualize the interesting questions and challenges raised by new technologies, rather than as an accurate description of a real place.

## see also...

Cyberpunk; Internet; Virtual reality

# Cyborg

An amalgamation of 'cybernetics' and 'organism', the term 'cyborg' was introduced by the Austrian neuroscientist Manfred Clynes at the beginning of the 1960s, to describe the need for humans to enhance their bodies technologically in order to survive in space. Whereas Clynes conceptualized humans with technologically-enhanced hearts and oxygen tanks, the notion of the cyborg has since been broadened to refer to any symbiosis of human and machine. On one level a cyborg is now seen as part-human and part-machine, as popularly portrayed in the science fiction films such as *Terminator* and *Robocop*. On a more practical level, around ten per cent of the population could be classed as cyborgs in the sense that they have medical technologies such as pacemakers or artificial heart valves inserted in their bodies. At its broadest level of use, the term is sometimes used to refer to humans who depend on any form of technology during their day-to-day life. From this metaphorical perspective, even computer game players and Internet users could be seen as cyborgs (at least temporarily).

Cyborg technologies can fulfil different objectives. They can be used in restorative or normalizing ways – for example, replacing deficient or lost parts of the body. Or they can be used to reconfigure or enhance humans to function beyond the current limitations of the human body. It is these latter categories of cyborgs to which many people are drawn – with the notion of 'post-humans' that are enhanced by technology no longer considered to be purely the domain of science fiction, despite the rudimentary nature of such technology at present.

At the moment the major significance of 'cyborg' is as a conceptual idea rather than a description of reality. As such, the notion of the cyborg has been used as a means to discuss the changing relationships between biological organisms and technology. A lot of this debate centres around the idea of humans using technology to take control of their bodies and redefine their day-to-day lives and identities. As a rather futuristic and abstract philosophical notion, the 'cyborg' raises some important issues for information technology and people.

## see also...

Cyberfeminism

# *Data*

In its purest sense, data refers to numbers, characters and other symbols which can be stored, accessed and manipulated by either humans or machines. Computers almost always represent data in terms of binary (ones and zeros). The term data is also used to distinguish machine-readable binary information from other forms of information, such as human-readable textual or alpha-numeric information, graphics, speech and images. Thus, we sometimes talk of data files and text files. In IT systems, data have no meaning until they are interpreted by a data processing system. In everyday life, data have no meaning until they are processed by humans.

In this sense, data can be seen as the building blocks of information and knowledge. Something has to be done to 'raw data' before they can be of use to either humans or machines – hence the need for data processing. Once some sort of meaning and context can be added to a piece of data it then becomes information. Information therefore carries an additional meaning above and beyond its symbols. For example, whereas '123' is data, 'I am driving a car at 123 miles per hour' is information. Information can then be collected, contextualized and enhanced, until it becomes useful knowledge (e.g. 'I am driving at 123 miles per hour which is illegal in this country'). A further level above this would be understanding, where knowledge is analysed, synthesized and built upon to create new knowledge (e.g. 'As I am driving at 123 miles per hour I should slow down to prevent getting arrested').

Thus, on its own, data are of little use without the requisite means to convert them into information and then knowledge. It is only then that we can decide whether the information derived from data is misconceived or even blatantly false. This distinction lies at the heart of the debates surrounding the utility of technologies such as the world wide web. Although the world wide web contains a vast amount of data and information on, for example, world economies, merely having access to the web does not necessarily make you knowledgeable about world economics (even assuming that this 'information' is correct). Knowledge and understanding involve some form of human processing and social contextualization – something that IT alone cannot provide.

## see also...

*Binary; Digital; Information*

# Data structure

A data structure is a software-based form of organized data storage, affecting how the data items are stored and retrieved. Thus, a file and the records in it could both be termed data structures, as could the fields within them. However, the term is usually reserved for more complex formal structures such as arrays, lists, queues, stacks and trees.

An array is a table or matrix. In most high level programming languages each array has its own variable name. Each cell within this variable stores a data element, and its position is defined by one or more subscripts. A one-dimensional array is simply a list, needing only one subscript to identify each cell. For example:

```
WHILE x VARIES FROM 1 to 1000
DISPLAY table(x)
ENDWHILE
```

This code might print the contents of a list of 1000 items in turn. This is much simpler and more efficient in terms of program coding than displaying 1000 separate variables. A two-dimensional array is like a table with rows and columns. Arrays can have any number of dimensions, but it is hard for programmers to visualize tables in more than three dimensions. Arrays, like

stacks, are static structures. They are of fixed size, and do not move around in memory. This means that data elements can be contiguous in memory, and that the elements themselves need not store any information about the structure (all of this is held in a header record).

Linked lists, queues and trees, on the other hand, are dynamic data structures. This gives them greater flexibility in use, but makes them harder to implement. As they change both in size and the range of memory that they use, special memory management techniques are required. Each data element in the structure also holds structural information, such as a pointer to the next element in sequence, that therefore need not be in the adjacent memory location. A queue works on the basis of first-in first-out. As data items are stored they are added to the back of the queue, and as they are used they are taken from the front. This means that either the queue moves slowly across a sequence of memory locations, or each item is copied into the next free space in turn every time an item is removed from the front. This is very wasteful of processor time.

see also...

Memory; Stack

# *Digital*

The idea of digital information lies at the heart of how information technologies function. At a basic level 'digital' refers to discontinuous data, based on the two distinct states of 'on' or 'off' (or 1 and 0) with no in-between. Digital computers, for example, are only capable of distinguishing between these two values of 0 and 1, but using binary codes are able to combine these zeros and ones into large numbers and other practical forms of information.

In order to understand what is so special about digital data, it is important to also understand its complement – analogue data. Analogue data can be measured as a continuously varying value. The most commonly cited example of analogue data is the hands of a clock that, by moving continuously around the clockface, provide an ongoing measurement of time. A digital clock, in comparison, is only capable of presenting a discontinuous series of numbers denoting time with a gap between each value (every one-hundredth of a second, for example). This distinction between digital and analogue may appear subtle but it is important. Humans generally experience the real world in analogue form. For example, vision is a response to the ever changing intensity and wavelengths of light. Similarly, sound is made when objects vibrate producing continually fluctuating pressure waves that can be picked up by our ears. Nevertheless, as our example of the digital clock suggests, most analogue events can be simulated through digital information.

So why then does modern-day IT privilege digital information over analogue? Firstly, digital information is far easier to store and distribute electronically. It is dense and compressible, meaning that a lot of digital data can be stored in a small physical space. Moreover, digital data are easier to manipulate accurately than 'real-world' analogue data. However, one aesthetic disadvantage of digital representation is that digital is always just an approximation of real sound or images (though the approximation may be very close). It can therefore be argued that vital 'natural' qualities are lost in the precise process of digitization.

*see also...*

*Binary; Data*

# Digital divide

As information technology becomes a more important means of accessing a wide range of information and services, some commentators have become concerned over emerging inequalities in IT access between different sections of society. The last ten years have therefore seen growing debate over the emergence of a gap between 'information haves' and 'information have-nots', popularly characterized by the media and politicians as the 'digital divide'.

Concern over the digital divide was first voiced with regard to inequalities in access to technology between 'developed' and 'developing' nations. Disparities between countries' levels of access to IT continue to be marked, leading some commentators to point to the emergence of the 'fourth world' of people; regions and countries so technologically marginalized that they are completely detached from the information age. The scale of this worldwide digital divide is highlighted by the fact that over half the world's population do not even have access to a basic telephone line – let alone a computer – suggesting the naivety of seeing IT as a 'global' phenomenon.

More recently, concerns have also grown over digital divides within countries. For example, in countries such as the UK and USA, despite rising levels of ownership of technologies such as home computers, the Internet and digital television, significant inequalities of access persist in terms of social class, income, gender, level of education, age, geography and ethnicity. Although some technologists are keen to dismiss such uneven patterns as merely reflecting 'early adopters' of technology, whose levels of technology use are eventually matched by the majority of the population, there is very strong evidence that these inequalities are strengthening over time rather than being reduced.

Yet the notion of the digital divide should not be seen merely in terms of access to new technologies – it is also evident in terms of people's experience of using IT, the availability of support and resources that people have available, as well as the quality and capability of the technology to which people have access. Thus, the digital divide is a complex social problem, and one that looks set to remain throughout future technological developments.

## see also...

Universal access

# E-

As a prefix to a host of words 'e-' has emerged over the last ten years to symbolize the application of information technology to human activities and enterprise. Originating with the use of e-mail, 'e-' denotes 'electronic' and has now been applied to almost all areas of life that entail some degree of technological application. Thus, we now hear reference to e-commerce, e-government, e-libraries, e-learning, e-publishing, as well as more esoteric activities such as e-therapy and e-religion. The prefix is currently widely used by businesses, the media and governments when referring to the use of telecommunications technologies, computers and other digital and electronic applications in daily life. More specific variations include 'i-' (referring to the Internet) 'cyber-' (referring to networked computers) and 'm-' (referring to mobiles).

The addition of 'electronic' to such activities is generally used to imply a technological improvement of a previously non-technological activity. Despite this it is far from clear that e-learning, for example, where students study interactively at a distance rather than face-to-face, actually presents such an improvement. In this way, the use of the 'e-' prefix is a good example of the societal marketing of information technology. As with the emergence of 'information and communications technology' (ICT), 'e-' stems from a wish to stress the convergence of computing and telecommunications technology, in particular the Internet. Whereas information and telecommunications technology has been applied to areas such as business, education and government over the last two decades, 'e-commerce', 'e-learning' and 'e-government' somehow denote 'new' and improved forms of these activities. Yet in practice, 'e-'activity can refer to a range of ICT-based activities, ranging from merely publishing information or interacting with customers and citizens on-line, to actually carrying out transactions and delivering products and services via ICT.

*see also...*

*E-commerce; Information and communications technology*

# E-commerce

An abbreviation of electronic commerce, 'e-commerce' is a widely used phrase referring to the carrying out of business via computer networks such as the Internet, opposed to conventional 'face-to-face' or paper-based methods. One popular manifestation of e-commerce is the buying and selling of goods on-line – referred to as 'e-tailing'. In fact, at the moment much e-commerce is little more than Internet-based mail order. Yet proponents argue that 'e-tailing' offers consumers more choice and more competitive pricing structures than can be achieved by conventional shop-based retailing. This principle can be seen in the book, video and software e-tailer 'amazon.com' – one of the few successful (and profitable) examples of e-tailing to date. Less successful but more innovative examples of e-tailing include on-line auctions and collective bulk-purchasing, where consumers around the globe combine forces to purchase goods at cheaper prices than would be possible on an individual basis. Aside from not being able to see or sample the products before purchase (as well as the ultimate reliance on postal delivery of goods), one of the main reasons behind current consumer reluctance to embrace e-tailing is the security of transactions. The need to provide details of credit card or bank account details when purchasing goods on-line has proved a major consumer deterrent. In order to overcome this barrier, technologists have been attempting to develop forms of 'digital cash', issued by banks and representing real money, that can be used on-line, although this is yet to be widely adopted.

E-commerce extends beyond e-tailing to other business activities. As well as facilitating B2C (business to consumer) contacts, computer networks are seen as important in increasing B2B (business to business) and B2G (business to government) interaction in terms of carrying out on-line business transactions and other communications. Much of this activity derives from the development of 'electronic data interchange' allowing companies to buy and sell information to each other. Given the rise of information as a key form of capital in the 'information economy', the number of firms who now conduct most of their business on-line is increasing, especially in sectors traditionally reliant on information as opposed to physical goods (such as the financial sector).

*see also...*

E-

# Edutainment

A combination of education and entertainment, the phrase 'edutainment' has existed since the early 1990s, originating from television production in much the same way as 'infomercials'. Referring to products, usually produced by commercial companies, that combine education and entertainment, edutainment has moved from describing television programmes such as Sesame Street and Teletubbies, to multimedia IT software. With the ever increasing sales of home computers to parents anxious to augment their child's learning, the edutainment software market is now seen as one of the fastest growing IT sectors.

Although it may appear rather bland as a concept, edutainment raises some fundamental questions surrounding IT and education. In particular, the rise of edutainment is a manifestation of the freedom that IT gives parents and children over when and where learning takes place. Whereas teaching and learning was traditionally the domain of the school and the teacher, information technologies now offer the opportunity for a kind of 'education in the home' from a variety of expert sources. This freedom of choice has led some commentators to argue that the Internet will lead to the 'death of schooling', as more and more parents will choose alternative sources of education via IT. Others counter that much of the available IT-based learning is of limited educational value and that edutainment software should be seen more as entertainment than a serious learning provision.

The rise of edutainment software is also symbolic of the creeping commercialism of IT-based education. With educational computing now a multi-billion dollar market, growing numbers of firms are getting involved in providing IT-based learning to parents and children. The argument here centres around whether private interests such as IT firms are capable of delivering education (seen as a fundamental public good) to all children on an equitable basis. With IT firms now charging considerable sums of money for educational software, the concern is that it will widen inequalities between those children whose parents can afford IT-based learning and those who must rely solely on school learning.

# E-mail

**E**-mail, or electronic mail, refers to the transmission of messages over computerized communication networks. These networks can either be local networks within organizations or, more popularly, networks with access to other computer systems enabling users to send e-mail on a worldwide scale. Indeed, the global reach of the Internet has precipitated a vast growth in the use of e-mail over the last decade – with billions of e-mail messages now sent and received around the world every year. A key characteristic of e-mail is that it is asynchronous. In other words, users can type messages which are electronically transmitted to recipients who can read, reply, print, forward or file them at their leisure. Crucially, the recipient does not have to be logged on to their computer at the time the message is sent in order to receive it. It is this feature of e-mail that has proved so popular with computer users.

Despite its relatively recent rise to prominence, e-mail has existed in various forms for over 40 years. During the 1960s, many companies and universities with mainframe computers and networked terminals used e-mail facilities so users could send messages to each other. As companies began to expand their computer systems to overseas offices, inter-employee e-mailing took on a worldwide dimension. At the end of the 1960s, the development of ARPAnet by the US military – now seen as the forerunner to the Internet – also involved the development of e-mail, with the first message sent in 1971. Since then the development of the Internet and other network systems has given rise to the rapid growth of e-mail as a form of communication.

One of the key debates surrounding e-mail is its impact on how people communicate with others. Whilst some critics bemoan its supposed detrimental effects on spelling and literacy, others celebrate the democratization of exchange that e-mail offers – arguing that the lack of social cues and hierarchical signifiers that usually dictate face-to-face communication leads to equality of opportunity and reciprocity in roles. As with all computer mediated communication, e-mail should be seen as a different, rather than superior, form of communication.

## see also...

Computer mediated communication

# Engelbart, Douglas

**D**ouglas Engelbart (born 1925) is an often overlooked pioneer of modern information technology, having developed much of what we now take for granted when using computers. Working at the Stanford Research institute in the USA, Engelbart has spent his life focusing on how humans and organizations can best use information technology to solve problems – thus making some of the defining advances in the field of Human Computer Interaction.

During the 1960s, Engelbart became interested in developing computer systems which allowed groups of workers to collaborate with each other regardless of distance or time. Now commonly referred to as groupware, Engelbart's work on 'computer supported co-operative work' led to the design of integrated computer-based environments which relied on visual interaction between the user and machine. Although the idea of visual interaction with a computer seems natural today, at the time the vast majority of computer programming and use was still being carried out by punched cards and paper tape. This newer approach led to the development of software applications such as shared screen teleconferencing, word processing, e-mail, hypertext and on-line help systems. Engelbart and his team were also largely responsible for the design of the mouse, windows and a rudimentary keyboard system – all integral features of the modern-day personal computer.

Engelbart's pioneering achievements have now led many people to take his later work seriously – hoping that this proves to be equally as influential. Here Engelbart has been focusing on 'bootstrapping' – an engineering principle where the results of an action are immediately fed back into the system to have a greater effect over a shorter time span and with less effort. Applying this principle to organizations, Englebart's recent work has concentrated on using technology and work structures to 'bootstrap' what he calls the 'collective IQ' of groups. Englebart is particularly interested in how new technologies such as the world wide web, groupware and 'open hyperdocument systems' will enable bootstrapping communities to thrive.

*see also...*

**Human Computer Interaction**

# Error propagation

**N**umbers are generally represented using a fixed word-length on a computer or electronic calculator, and this limits the number of decimal places or significant figures that can be represented. In most cases this does not matter (when we are working only with whole numbers, for example). However, when we restrict the accuracy of the numbers we work with by using a computer, or via approximation in a real-life measurement, we introduce representational errors. The number held in the computer may not be exactly the same as the real-life figure, although the difference will be very small. The important question is what happens to this inaccuracy as the figure involved is used in arithmetic operations? How does the error propagate?

We tend to behave as though any small error component in our analysis remains constant, so that if we start with figures at a certain level of accuracy, we will end up with results at approximately the same level of accuracy. In some cases this belief may be appropriate but in others it is not so. If we assume that all of our measurements are slightly in error, then adding two figures also involves adding their error components. The error components may partly cancel

each other out, or they may increase each other. This can be seen if we imagine two numbers whose true value is A and B, for which our measurements a and b are only approximations, such that $a = (A + E_a)$ and $b = (B + E_b)$, where $E_a$ is the error in our measurement of A, and $E_b$ the error in B. If we add our estimates of A and B we actually reach the sum $a + b$ (equal to $A + B + E_a + E_b$). This is unlikely to be a major problem since the proportion $(E_a + E_b)/(A + B)$ is probably not much larger than either $E_a$ /A or $E_b$ /B (i.e. the proportionate errors with which we started). Since we do not know whether $E_a$ and $E_b$ are positive or negative, the same result occurs when we subtract A and B. However, if we multiply a by b we obtain $(A + E_a) \times (B + E_b)$ which equals $(A \times B) + (B \times E_a) + (A \times E_b) + (E_a \times E_b)$ (and similarly for division). The error term $B \times E_a$ could be large if B is very large. For some problems, the introduction of an error component makes a large difference, and sometimes *all* of the difference.

*see also...*

*Corruption; Floating point*

# Execution cycle

The execution cycle (or fetch-execute cycle) is the sequence of actions performed within the central processing unit between each clock pulse, to carry out one machine instruction. The execution cycle involves deciding on the next instruction to be carried out, fetching it from memory, executing it, and adjusting the necessary registers in time for the next cycle. The basic nature of this cycle is the same on all digital computers of whatever make and size, and the cycle continues for as long as the computer is switched on. Each step in the cycle is initiated by control signals (on/off) sent from the control unit, which open or close pathways within the central processing unit. When information is transferred within the central processing unit it is sent along all potentially available routes, but only the destination register also receives a control signal. Entry to the register is only possible with the signal *and* the data.

More formally the common steps are as follows:

1 Release Program Counter contents to address bus – causing contents of specified memory location to be copied to the data bus
2 Release contents of data bus to Instruction Register
3 Increment Program Counter (to point to next memory location in sequence)
4 Execute instruction in Instruction Register
5 Return to step 1.

When the performance of a computer is described in terms of a frequency, this refers to the execution cycle and thus to the number of instructions carried out per second. For example, four megaHertz means that the computer can carry out 4,000 cycles per second. When there is a branch or jump within the program, meaning that the next instruction to be executed is not the next one in sequence, a new value (the destination of the jump) is moved into the program counter. When the program is interrupted by the operating system, the cycle itself is undisturbed, but the address of the first instruction in the operating system is placed in the program counter. Thus, on the next cycle the central processing unit starts running the operating system automatically, instead of the previous program.

## see also...

*Central processing unit; Interrupt; Memory*

# File access

Files can be designed for access in a variety of ways. Each has advantages, which is why most systems use a variety of formats.

Serial access only allows data in the form of records to be written to, or read from, the file in sequence. This is particularly suitable for batch processing operations using magnetic tape. A key concept here is the hit ratio. If the ratio of records to be used (hit) in one application is high in comparison to the total number of records then serial access is the most efficient. In payroll calculations, the hit-rate is usually 100 per cent as every employee has a record and everyone gets paid. It takes less storage space and time to process if the employee records are simply placed in series (by name or employee number) and dealt with in turn.

Direct access allows data to be directly written to, or read from, the file in any order. This is particularly useful for real-time operations using magnetic disc packs, where the hit-rate is low. A product database might be used on-line by customers to find records relating to the current price of a particular product. Users will not want to wait while the file is read from the beginning until it finds the record for the product they want. Instead they use a key (such as

the product number). The key is hashed – converted via arithmetic into an address in the range of the file – and the address in terms of cylinder (track) and sector (block) is used to find the desired record on disc. Note that direct access is somewhat different from random, because all searches are *not* constant length (due to variations in seek time and rotational latency on the disc), and because of the nature of hashing there will be some overflow records.

Perhaps the most flexible format is indexed sequential access. This is suitable for applications where the hit-rate is very variable. A library catalogue system may be used to check the availability of an individual book and sometimes processed in entirety to print out all outstanding reminders. It would not be efficient to use two different versions of the file. A solution is to store the records in sequence, so that they can be processed serially, but to index them so that the key is used to look up the disc address of each record. It takes more storage space than serial access and is slower than direct access.

see also...

Memory; Storage device

# *File security*

With large amounts of data in computer-based files, security is a major issue. Security does not usually refer to protection of the data from theft or espionage, which is most easily dealt with by physical security and password identities. File security more commonly refers to safety from loss or damage.

Many of the same procedures that would be used for manual filing still apply to computer-based filing. Everything should have an external label of contents (to prevent over-writing), an expiry date, and particularly important items could be kept in a fire-proof safe. However, the nature of computer files allows a range of additional measures. It is easier to copy electronic data than to copy paper, so there is no good reason for files not to be regularly 'backed-up'. This can be done intermittently, by copying all files at the end of the day or incrementally, by copying only changes since the last full back-up. It goes without saying that the copy should not be kept in the same place or on the same medium as the original. In a batch processing system, files will be updated intermittently and no additional security is needed. The original versions of the file (the master) and the file of recent changes (the transactions) can be merged to generate the new file. The new file becomes the live file, while the old ones are stored as backup (and can be used to regenerate the new file if it is lost). This is known as the generation of files, or the grandfather/father/son method.

Other methods of security include write-permit rings and internal labels. Internal labels are the file header records that identify the contents of the file and warn the operator against over-writing if the expiry date has not been reached. Most storage devices include something like the write-permit ring, so that they are set to read data only. In order to alter the file using these devices the operator must manually override the defaults. Floppy discs have a switch at the top left rear. If the switch is set to create a hole in the cover then writing is not permitted on that disc, so important files can be protected from accidental erasure. Breakable tabs on an audio cassette perform a similar function.

## see also...

*Corruption; Storage devices; Verification and validation*

# Floating point

**W**e are used to working with fixed point numbers where the number is assumed to be an integer, unless there is an explicit decimal point. This is because we do not generally work with very large or very small numbers. When we do, perhaps using a calculator, the screen is not large enough to accommodate the leading or trailing zeroes. In this case it is conventional to use floating point form, expressing numbers in two parts such as '3.456 E13'. The first part is known as the mantissa, and consists of as many significant digits as the display allows. The second part is known as the exponent, and expresses the magnitude of the number. Our example is 3.456 times ten to the power of 13, or 34,560,000,000,000.

A very similar process is used inside computers (in binary) to represent and store real numbers. If the mantissa is positive then the number is positive overall, otherwise it is negative. The mantissa itself has a fixed point, often after the first (sign) bit. If the exponent is positive the number is large, and if it is negative the number is a fraction. Since the number is binary, the exponent expresses a power of two (rather than ten). In a simple system in which each part uses one byte and all numbers are in two's complement form, the range of numbers would be as follows:

- the largest number would be
  0.1111111 01111111
  (which is +127/128 times two to the power of +127, or approximately 1.69 times $10^{+38}$)
- the smallest number would be
  1.0000000 01111111
  (which is −1 times two to the power of +127, or approximately -1.70 times $10^{+38}$)
- the smallest positive number would be 0.1000000 10000000
  (which is +1/2 times two to the power of −128, or approximately 6.81 times $10^{-38}$).

In the last example, the mantissa cannot be smaller than one half since floating point numbers are always stored in a normalized form with the first significant digit after the point. Therefore, the first two bits of the mantissa are always opposites, and this knowledge can be used as an error check. If, as a result of arithmetic, the number becomes too large to be represented it overflows (and is treated as an error), and if too small it underflows (and is treated as zero).

*see also...*

**Binary; Error propagation**

# Futurology

The need to assess accurately the potential impacts of technology on society is a vital part of attempting to manage and control technology. The last 80 years have seen a rise in 'technological forecasting', in particular a popularist strand of technology assessment that has become known as 'futurology'. Futurology is the study of current trends in order to forecast future developments. It is often speculative in nature, but is nevertheless important as it has had an influence on public perceptions of issues such as information technology and the 'information society'.

Indeed, both concepts first came to the attention of many people through the work of futurologists such as Alvin Toffler, Tom Stonier and others. Throughout the 1970s and 1980s, various optimistic visions of technology-led new eras became best sellers – a trend repeated in a similar rash of writing in the Internet-obsessed 1990s. Whilst it is easy to dismiss these accounts of new technology-based societies as fanciful and popularist, early futurology such as Alvin Toffler's *Future Shock* and *The Third Wave* introduced many of the key aspects of the information society discourse to wider audiences. For example, via his discussion of 'techno-rebels' and 'telecommuters', the rise of the 'prosumer' and the 'crack-up of the nation', Toffler highlighted many issues that were at the heart of the information society debate.

The popularity of such writing is not always based on its status as an accurate and balanced view of the technological future. Criticism of futurology has centred mainly on the limitations of its models and the subjective, interpretative nature of projections based on them. In particular, many accounts in futurology of the inevitability of technological 'progress' reflect implicit technological determinism. We need to be conscious, therefore, of who is making such predictions and what their motivations may be for doing so. Much futurology is driven by an ideological or political desire to see 'better' forms of society. Thus, technology is often used by futurologists as a means through which idealized societies can be created – hence the utopian nature of much futurology, that is prescriptive rather than predictive.

## see also...

Technological determinism

# Fuzzy logic

**W**hereas computers are very effective machines at carrying out repetitive and highly defined tasks, the problem of getting them to 'think', 'reason' and 'act' like humans has proved difficult, and forms the basis for the field of 'artificial intelligence'. One of the main reasons for the 'inhuman' nature of computers' thinking is their reliance on traditional forms of Boolean logic which are based around absolute states of false/true, on/off, yes/no, 0/1, etc. These forms of logic do not allow for more imprecise notions such as 'fairly', 'very' and 'quite' that humans use regularly and easily in their own reasoning.

Fuzzy logic is therefore a form of logic designed for the representation of linguistically 'soft' notions that cannot be defined precisely but depend on their context (such as hot/cold, short/tall, light/dark). For example, a stick may be described as being too long *or* too short depending on whether it is to be used as a toothpick or a flagpole. In practice, fuzzy logic works by using a multi-valued logic instead of a binary logic. Instead of relying on the two traditional truth values of 'true' and 'false', a fuzzy logic program may assign values to states of 'partial truth' between 'completely true' and 'completely false', such as 'fairly true', 'not very true' and 'fairly false'. Thus, relative notions are still denoted by real numbers but with a greater degree of latitude.

In theory, fuzzy logic can enable computers to respond more like humans to complex stimuli. One practical manifestation of this has been the development of 'fuzzy' controllers, where a rule-based controller can be developed using rules such as 'if the speed gets very fast then slightly reduce the pressure'. Converted into a fuzzy logic algorithm, the computer is then capable of acting on these relative rules. Many fuzzy control applications are used today in consumer products such as washing machines, video cameras, and cars. However, even in the area of fuzzy control, the ability of computers to 'reason' like humans is limited. This is because the fuzzy rules (and therefore the understanding of the context of the action) are originally derived from expert human controllers and the tasks that they are applied to could be considered mundane and repetitive by human standards.

## see also...
### Artificial intelligence

# Garbage in, garbage out

This is a long established principle of data processing, but one which is still often overlooked by many computer users. Put simply, the result of any computer-aided procedure is never any better than the quality of the programs and data given to it. While this is a seemingly obvious proposition, and one that most people would apply readily away from a technological setting, it appears to become forgotten when computers are involved. Whether this is due to a misplaced notion of computer initiative or intelligence, it is the case that people can give undue weight to computer-generated output. Computer printout has considerable rhetorical power.

You will meet this in several guises. Suppose a dispute arises about the answer to an arithmetic problem. If one 'solution' was hand-calculated and the other machine-calculated then more often than not it is the latter that will be favoured. In fact, what the divergent results show you is that there is an error somewhere. It could be an arithmetic slip, but it could also be an error in entering the relevant values into the computer. There is no reason, *a priori*, to privilege the machine-generated result. A more subtle version of the same trend can be experienced when people complain that 'the computer will not let us do this' or when excusing a mistake by blaming the computer. A travel agent might get into the habit of routinely altering the totals printed on invoices because the software is in error and it ignores a key factor (an insurance premium perhaps). When asked by customers why they do this they answer that there is nothing to worry about – but that the computer is making a mistake. Comments such as this deny the 'garbage in, garbage out' principle, and perhaps lead us to imagine that it does not apply to technology.

Garbage is also used as a term to apply to obsolete data, particularly on backing storage. When the operating system re-packages the data files on a disc system to maximize free space, it routinely deletes unwanted data items, often left in spaces between live files. This is called garbage collection.

see also...

*Corruption; Error propagation*

39

# Global village

The media theorist Marshall McLuhan first coined the phrase 'global village' to describe the effect of electronic media such as radio and television in bringing people into closer and more immediate contact with others around the world. Although McLuhan originally wrote about the global village in the 1960s, the concept has become increasingly popular over the last decade with the rise of the Internet. Now the global village is seen to be an accurate prediction of Internet-based society, where everybody is perceived to have contact with everybody else, regardless of national boundaries, making us members of a global community. Proponents of the global village often talk of people as being free roaming 'Netizens' as opposed to citizens tied down to physical countries. The notion of the global village has also caught the imagination of politicians and business people, with government policies and commercial products regularly being promoted as helping create the 'global village'. Given the radical nature of McLuhan's original ideas, the widespread acceptance and use of the global village idea often ignores the fundamental points that McLuhan was trying the make – in particular, new technologies leading to a welcome return to tribalism and primivatism.

McLuhan bemoaned the fact that over the centuries, human beings had been conditioned to accept certain senses as more important than others. He argued that in the primitive, tribal world, people were far more reliant on all the senses, especially touch, taste, hearing and smell. Yet over time, sight had been privileged over all the other senses by the rise of the written word and the phonetic alphabet. McLuhan saw the dominance of sight as leading to a detribalization of the Western world in specialized societies. The storage and hierarchical classification of information and the rise of technologies such as the printing press had all led to an increasing fragmentation of people into separate countries and individual communities. However, McLuhan reasoned that electronic media were leading to a rebalancing of the senses with new technologies such as the television, radio and telephone, re-introducing the need for hearing and touch alongside sight, and therefore facilitating a return towards tribalized society.

see also...

*Time-space compression*

# Hackers

Hackers, and the art of hacking, refer to people who enjoy the mastering of computer programming and are considered to have expert knowledge in the area, differing from conventional users of IT who generally learn only a basic repertoire of skills in order to 'get by'. Hackers, on the other hand, are seen inherently to enjoy the challenge of mastering all aspects of computer programming, often for its own sake, and are sometimes employed to develop software and overcome programming problems. However, the term 'hacker' is often also used in a different light by the media to refer to computer programmers who intentionally breach computer security and break into computer systems with the intention of causing disruption. People behind these activities are more accurately referred to as 'crackers' and many hackers are at pains to distance their legitimate interest in gaining knowledge about computer systems from the 'breaking and entering' activities of crackers.

As expert programmers responsible for the development of computer programming over the last 40 years, there is a strong shared culture among hackers which reflects a liberal belief in the sharing of computer knowledge. Many programmers subscribe to the ethic that information sharing is a positive good and that it is their ethical duty to develop open-source software which can be given away to other computer users. This 'hacker ethic' can be best seen in the vast co-operative networks of computer programmers sharing technical expertise and resources across the Internet.

Yet, despite this emphasis on individual freedom and collective collaboration, hackers can be seen as constituting a very restricted group of computer users. Ironically, their extreme involvement with computers and their desire to separate themselves from 'mainstream' computer users, leaves hackers as a very closed and non-inclusive counter-culture in IT. This privileging of computer expertise can be seen as restrictive in widening the appeal of IT. This has been argued to be particularly pertinent to the enduring gender-imbalance in the IT industry, with the extremely masculinized and competitive 'hacker' culture often seen as a deterrent to female computer programmers from aspiring to become expert programmers themselves.

*see also...*

*Cyberpunk*

# Hardware

In essence, the hardware of any computer or communication system consists of those parts that you can kick (or more accurately that you can touch). It is, therefore, the equipment, circuits, recording media and such-like of a computer. This is usually contrasted with the software, such as the programs and data, and sometimes also with what technologists refer to as the 'liveware' or people, such as users and operators. The hardware typically consists of a central processing unit (the basis of the computer itself), the peripheral devices (for storing data and communicating with the outside world) and related media such as floppy discs or CD-ROMs. Since the hardware is visible it tends to form the basis of many people's estimate of the cost of buying a computer, whereas a computer is often a 'puppy-dog sale', with the cost of software, communication and maintenance eventually dwarfing the cost of the hardware itself.

Hardware can also refer to the circuitry in any equipment, and this has undergone a revolution since the introduction of the microprocessor in the 1970s. Whereas any piece of equipment used to have to be hard-wired to perform its function – with toasters, washing machines and air conditioners each having their own specialist circuit

design – it is now commonplace for the control functions of any piece of equipment to be based on a microprocessor. While this is still hardware, its specific function in any device is determined by the software, for a microprocessor is essentially a small programmable computer (often on one chip). This has two major advantages for the manufacturer. Firstly, although a microprocessor is more sophisticated than a dedicated electronic circuit, if it is the only circuit needed in a range of devices then it is cheaper to produce. Secondly, if the functions need changing, it can be done at the software level only, with no need to do any traditional re-engineering of the electronics at all.

Accordingly, by the 1980s, the microprocessor was being hailed as the last ever electronic circuit, capable of being programmed to perform 'any' function, and so heralding a new era of electronics in which the implementation of a design did not involve dealing with the hardware at all.

---

*see also...*

*Central processing unit;*
*Peripherals; Software*

# *Hopper, Grace*

**R**ear Admiral Dr Grace Hopper (1906–92) was a ground-breaking computer programmer and also a pioneering woman in the development of information technology. Like Ada Lovelace before her, Hopper came to work on computers as a programmer but ended up developing some of the operating techniques that define modern-day computer use.

Hopper was drafted to the US Naval Reserve in 1943. Given her previous employment as a professor of mathematics, she was posted to Harvard University. There she worked on the Mark I computing machine and was only the third person assigned to program it. Hopper went on to develop the programming techniques of the Mark I, II and III machines as well as producing a 500-page manual of operations for the Automatic Sequence-Controlled Calculator, where she outlined some of the fundamental principles of computer programming.

One of Hopper's growing obsessions was with making computing more accessible to non-mathematicians. To this end she then began working on a technique that became known as a compiler. Her A-O series of compilers translated symbolic mathematical code that humans could understand, into the binary code instructions that computers could understand (machine code). This was achieved by giving different call numbers to a series of programming routines that were stored on a magnetic tape. This allowed the programmer to tell the computer what to do via a simple call number, instead of inputting the lengthy instructions in binary form. Its initial success led Hopper to explore the use of English language commands instead of numbers in computer programs. Her development of the B-O (or FlowMatic) compiler which could 'understand' and act on 20 English commands was the forerunner to modern-day computer languages. However, at the time, Hopper's ideas were met with resistance by her peers who saw the computer as a purely mathematical machine. However, Hopper's work led to a range of techniques and developments which are now at the heart of modern-day computer programming, an achievement for which she was widely recognized in her lifetime.

---

*see also...*

*Lovelace, Ada; Programming language; Translation*

# Human Computer Interaction

As computers moved from being used chiefly in research laboratories and into general business settings, technologists found themselves having to pay increasing attention to human as well as technical factors when designing computer systems. In particular, the field of Human Computer Interaction (HCI) has emerged over the past 40 years as a significant area of information technology, concerned with studying how people interact with computers and, it follows, designing and evaluating interactive computer systems for human use. Given this broad brief, HCI spans different disciplines – from the technical perspectives of computer science and industrial design, to understanding the psychology of computer use and the social aspects of how IT fits into work and other organizational settings.

As a field of study, HCI is concerned with all aspects of people's use of IT, from the way hardware looks and feels, to the design and structuring of software. A growing area is in developing an understanding of how humans are cognitively and physiologically able to interact with computer systems, leading to the design of systems to meet these characteristics. HCI is also concerned with improving how humans and machines communicate with each other and, in particular, developing human/computer interfaces that have a high level of 'usability' but also remain functional. Typically, more than half a computer system's lines of program code may now be concerned with interacting with the user. Some of the most noticeable advances in computer design have been the development of graphical user interfaces such as the desktop metaphor inherent in the operating systems of many personal computers, as well as input devices such as the mouse and touch screen technology, all designed to make computers more intuitive to use and less reliant on technical expertise. Achieving an equitable balance between human ease of use and efficiency of system design is therefore the primary concern of HCI.

## see also...

Engelbart, Douglas

# *Hypertext*

ypertext is a non-linear way of presenting information on computers. Instead of the reader being forced to read a text in the sequential order that the author wrote it, readers of hypertext can follow their own direction through the text, choosing which segments of information they read and in which order. In this way, readers of hypertext are better able to create their own meaning from the presented material.

A hypertext document is created by providing 'links' within a segment of information which allow readers to then move or jump to associated segments of information. Although hypertext systems have been in use since the 1960s, the development of the world wide web facilitated the widespread use of hypertext-based information by computer users. Now the vast majority of information on web pages is presented in the form of hypertext. Crucially, a hypertext document can incorporate different forms of information, such as text, pictures, sound or video – also referred to as hypermedia.

The key defining features of hypertext are its non-linearity and the supposed control it gives the reader. Many commentators have gone as far as to argue that the growing use of hypertext will redefine traditional Western notions of literacy as a more 'naturalistic' way of presenting information for human brains. Human memory is seen to be associative and to work in several dimensions at once. Humans are therefore more adept at processing information that is presented in loose networks rather than in a rigid linear fashion. Whilst this may be true, the human mind also organizes and processes some information on a more linear, hierarchical basis. As hypertext relies on readers to organize the text for themselves, it can sometimes prove to be more difficult to process as effectively as 'traditional' text, and may therefore deter those whose traditional literacy is already limited. Hypertext is certainly important, as increasing amounts of information are being presented in this way across a range of technologies. However, to argue that it will lead to the death of linear text is a rather extreme view. Rather than heralding the redefinition of literacy, hypertext should be seen as an alternative form of presenting and organizing information.

*see also...*

**World wide web**

45

# IBM

IBM began life in 1911 as the Computer Tabulating Recording Company, producing clocks, scales and punch card tabulating machines. In 1914, it changed its name to International Business Machines (IBM) and began its long existence as the world's leading information technology company. Throughout the last century, IBM was largely responsible for developing and producing commercially a number of ground-breaking information technologies and associated applications; including the world's first supercomputers, fractal geometry and relational databases.

In popular conception, perhaps the defining technology that IBM was responsible for was the launch in 1981 of the IBM 'personal computer' or PC. IBM had been considering a move away from purely business machines into the growing personal computer market during the end of the 1970s and decided in 1980 to produce a small, single-user computer, built from off-the-shelf parts and distributed to domestic and business users through high street shops. The IBM PCs used Intel microchips, had a colour monitor and magnetic floppy disc drive and ran on an operating system called DOS, produced by a burgeoning software company called Microsoft. Crucially, IBM allowed other companies to produce replica PCs, known as 'clones', thus allowing 'IBM compatible' computers to flood the marketplace against the technically more innovative Apple computers. Aided by a famous marketing campaign using Charlie Chaplin's 'little tramp' character, the PC was an instant and enduring success.

Despite its market leader status, IBM has garnered an unenviable reputation among sections of the computer-using community. Many computer enthusiasts resent IBM's success as an omnipresent and monolithic IT company – arguing that its machines are now unsophisticated and unimaginatively designed. Hackers often deride IBM computers as unwieldy to use and designed primarily for the bland corporate business market. 'Big Blue', as the company is known, is often seen as anathema to 'real' computer users. Nevertheless, IBM's enduring domination of what is a notoriously volatile marketplace is testament to the robustness of its products. As the popular business saying goes, 'No one ever got sacked for buying IBM'.

*see also...*

*Apple; Hardware; Microsoft*

# *Information*

In Information theory, information is defined as something that reduces uncertainty. If several people apply for the same job and are told after the interviews who has got the job, then they have received some information. The importance of this definition is that it enables us to measure information in terms of the uncertainty that it replaces. The smallest unit of information would be that which decided between two alternatives (if only two people had applied for the job in the example above). This smallest unit of information is a binary digit, also known as a 'bit', and all other units of information can be expressed in terms of these bits.

Since one bit contains enough information to decide between two alternatives (0 or 1, on or off), then two bits in combination contain enough to decide between four alternatives (00, 01, 10, 11), three bits have eight combinations (000, 001, 010, 011, 100, 101, 110, 111) and so on. Thus, 10 bits can be used to create $2^{10}$ different numbers, where $2^{10}$ equals 1,024 (known colloquially as one K, for kilobit). Similarly $2^{20}$ equals 1,048,576 (known as one M, for megabit), while a gigabit (G) would be $2^{30}$, or just over 1 billion.

In practice, bits within computer designs are usually grouped into standard-sized clusters known as 'words', and the word-length of a computer is the number of bits (usually a multiple of eight) in the standard cluster for that computer type. This length will usually be the number of bits carried in parallel on the data and address buses in the central processing unit, the number of bits stored in each special register and each memory location, and also the number of bits used to represent each complete machine instruction. The longer the word-length of the computer the more work, in general, that it can perform in each execution cycle.

A byte (originally a very weak pun) is a group of eight bits, or enough information to represent one ASCII character. The byte is the unit in which manufacturers commonly express the size of the computer's main memory. A memory of four megabytes (4Mb) would therefore be capable of holding just over four million ASCII characters, while a memory of eight gigabytes (8Gb) would be able to hold just over eight billion letters, digits or symbols.

## see also...

*ASCII; Baud; Binary; Data*

# Information and communications technology

nformation and communications technology (ICT) is fast becoming the accepted term of reference for contemporary information technologies. ICT refers to a range of technological applications, such as computer hardware and software, digital broadcast technologies, and telecommunications technologies such as mobile phones and the Internet, as well as electronic information resources such as the world wide web and CD-ROMs.

In theory, the 'C' of ICT stresses both the 'C' of communication and the 'C' of convergence. ICT is therefore seen to be an updating of the conventional term 'information technology' (or IT) by highlighting the rapid convergence of technologies such as computers, telecommunications and broadcasting technologies, whilst also stressing the communicative and networking capacity of modern-day information technologies. But whilst technological convergence and technology-based communications are important developments to emphasize, both *could* be seen to be adequately covered by conventional definitions of information technology. Indeed, the term 'information technology' has long been taken to include telecommunications and other forms of information transfer, as well as referring to a range of technologies other than the computer.

This has led some technologists to question the need for the semantic switch from IT to ICT. Yet the promotion of ICT by governments and IT firms is largely of symbolic rather than practical significance. ICT came to prominence during the mid-1990s, when governments and the IT industry felt the need to promote the rapidly emerging Internet and 'information superhighway' to their citizens and consumers. At this point, IT had become too closely aligned as a term with the specific use of computers, and a string of unsuccessful applications such as videodiscs and miniature televisions. So we would be wise to treat ICT as little more than a political re-branding of IT, in the same way that IT was used to replace now long-abandoned terms such as micro-electronics and data-processing.

*see also...*

*Multimedia*

# Information society

The idea of the information society is an attempt to describe the changing technological and economic world in which we are living. In particular, the information society refers to a post-industrial society where the production and consumption of information and knowledge are now more important than traditional manufacturing and production of goods. The information society is therefore characterized by the rising importance of information and knowledge as key sources of power and competitiveness in the 'global economy'. Crucially, it is the growth of information technology that most people would see as leading to these changes.

Of course, as authors such as Manuel Castells argue, the idea of information and the communication of knowledge has been crucial in all societies. So our modern-day idea of the information society should be more accurately referred to as the '*informational society*'; where information generation, processing and transmission have become the fundamental sources of productivity and power because of the emergence of new technologies.

Such is the extent of these changes that the idea of the information society has been used to justify the need for fundamental change in countries around the world. For example, governments are now spending billions of pounds to adapt their economies to the needs of this information society. It is also frequently argued that all workers must now be trained in the use of technology and information because the nature of their employment is changing. Similarly, all firms are now being urged to embrace new technologies or otherwise perish.

Although the idea of the information society does refer to widespread changes, we must be careful not to see it as a 'new' kind of society. Not everyone's lives are being transformed by technology and many of the economic changes being forecasted appear wildly exaggerated. Thus, any talk of the information society 'revolution' should not be seen as a concrete forecast of how things *will* be, but rather as an idealized view of how things *could* be.

see also...

Information; Network society

# Information superhighway

The term 'information superhighway' was popularized by Vice President Al Gore in the early 1990s, when referring to the US Government's aim of creating a global communications network carrying data and information. As such, the term was an attempt to make political gain from the popular rise of the Internet at the time, although the two terms were not meant to be synonymous. The information superhighway was seen as specifically describing what governments and businesses could do with the Internet. It was a vision of a commercially and politically controlled information network, loosely based around the Internet and carrying business, government and educational information. However, such is the jargon-ridden nature of IT that there was soon much confusion between terms such as the 'information superhighway', the 'Internet' and 'cyberspace' (with Gore even apparently claiming in 2000 that his greatest achievement as vice president was to have 'invented the Internet'!).

Nevertheless, the idea of an information superhighway (or 'Infobahn' as it is sometimes referred to) encapsulates some of the key debates underlying the rise of information networks. In particular, the idea of 'building' an information superhighway was seen as the job of commercial companies, although it was acknowledged that they should be given initial support by governments. Thus, the US Government saw its role as encouraging the private sector to invest in information networks and to promote competition between firms, whilst also trying to ensure that every citizen could have access if they wished. However, concerns were expressed that companies would inevitably want to charge 'tolls' to use the information superhighway and therefore exclude some people from using it at all. The idea of the information superhighway was also treated with derision by existing Internet users who saw the Internet as a place that no government or company could claim to 'own' or 'control'. For these reasons alone, the notion of the information superhighway is becoming less frequently used by all but the most out-of-touch politicians.

see also...

*Cyberspace; Internet; National information infrastructure*

# Input device

An input device is a peripheral device used to transfer data from the external world into a computer system. It converts the data from its source form (the way in which it is represented originally) into a computer coded object form. In many cases, the source form is characters, such as those on the keys of a keyboard ('A', '*', '3' etc.), and the object form is a character code such as ASCII. The keyboard is probably the most prevalent input device, traditionally arranged in the 'QWERTY' order of its predecessor, the typewriter, that used this order of letters to stop the 'arms' of different characters physically jamming together. Different arrangements and styles of keyboard have been devised – alphabetical order, larger central keys for commonly used letters, pictorial keyboards and so on – but all of these have to overcome the obstacle of typists trained to use the standard QWERTY model who do not wish to unlearn their skill. The keyboard is prone to error in operation (I have made four mistakes in typing this sentence so far), slow to use, and is designed to use only alphanumeric data.

Input devices include the mouse, light pen, microphone, and touch-sensitive screen. Specialized examples include Magnetic Ink Character Readers (used to read cheque details in banking), Optical Character Readers (used in sorting mail by post-codes), Optical Mark Readers (used in scoring multiple-choice tests), bar code readers (used in supermarket checkouts) and voice recognition units.

Input to a computer is notoriously slow, since the number of characters per second that can be transferred into memory, even from the fastest input devices, is far less than the number that can be handled in the same time period by the central processing unit. Modern-day processors operate in thousands or millions of cycles per second, whereas input devices transfer data at a rate of less than one to hundreds of characters per second.

For this reason, the processor in many computer systems is not directly linked to input (or output) devices – that are therefore said to be 'off-line'. The processor is used for other tasks, while data is transferred from the input device to a dedicated section of memory called a buffer store.

*see also...*

ASCII; Baud

# *Interactivity*

Getting computer software to respond to, and interact with, human users is a vital element of contemporary IT, and a current obsession with software producers. At a broad level, interactivity in a computer program gives the user a degree of influence and control in their use of the program and, ultimately, in terms of the outcomes of using the program. Therefore, in some form or other, interactive computer programs are designed to give the user choices at regular intervals. Once the user has made his/her choice, the computer responds by carrying out the function to which the command referred. Pointing to and clicking on a program icon, for example, prompts the computer to begin to run the program. In this respect, interactivity is not a new concept in IT. Although some background (or batch) programs are designed to run without any immediate user involvement (such as virus protection software), most computer software involves an element of user input and system response. Now, graphical user interfaces such as the Windows operating system and hypertext-based environments such as the world wide web, offer users a huge range of interaction options. This idea is taken to the extreme by the development of virtual reality software, when the user is constantly interacting with the computer via touch, sight and voice.

Interactivity has grown in importance as multimedia software has become more sophisticated, allowing users potential access to thousands of different pieces of text, graphics and sound. Unless users can make choices to move around and access these different resources easily and effectively, the sophisticated content of the program is wasted. Therefore, interactivity defines users' experiences of modern multimedia software. However, offering users too many choices and too much interactivity can be disadvantageous. Interaction requires thought on the part of the user and overloading users with too many choices can result in disengagement with the program. Therefore, one of the key challenges facing software designers is achieving a desirable balance between setting defaults and offering users an optimum level of interactivity that does not become obtrusive or hamper the smooth use of a piece of software.

## see also...
*Batch/real-time; Virtual reality*

# *Internet*

The Internet is a global network connecting millions of computers, allowing them to communicate with each other via a series of software protocols or rules. 'Inter' refers to the international nature of the connections between computers and 'net' refers to network – hence the name Inter(national) net(work). Crucially, the worldwide connection of computers allows Internet users to exchange data with other Internet users. Examples of such Internet-based exchanges include on-line communication (such as e-mail and chat facilities), on-line conferencing (discussion lists and bulletin boards), distributed information resources (downloading information from the world wide web) as well as other forms of file transfer.

The Internet arose from ARPAnet – an American military network developed by the US Advanced Research Projects Agency during the late 1960s. The concept of ARPAnet was to produce a computer-based communications system that could continue to function in the event of a nuclear attack – a solution reached through the design of a decentralized rather than centralized network. During the 1970s and 1980s, the ARPAnet was used mainly by universities and research agencies with over 10,000 computers connected by 1987. When the APRA was disbanded in 1990, the system was superseded by the Internet.

The key feature of the Internet is that, unlike centrally controlled computer networks, it is decentralized by design. Each computer connected to the Internet is independent from all the others. Thus, operators of Internet-connected computers can choose which Internet services they use, as well as which services local to them they wish to make available to the wider Internet community. Every Internet-connected computer has the potential to be both a recipient and provider of information. It is this decentralized nature of the Internet that is seen by users and enthusiasts as its defining feature – with many people arguing that the unstructured and anarchic nature of the Internet leads to individual freedom. Yet, as key elements of the Internet become increasingly commercialized and fall under the control of large multinational companies, this democratic and idealistic view of the Internet may be under threat.

## *see also...*

*E-mail; World wide web*

# Interrupt

An interrupt is a return of control of a computer to its operating system. It is a signal that some part of the system requires attention, detected by the central processing unit as the presence of a flag in the processor status register. Therefore, the program currently being executed is suspended, the address in the program counter is placed on the stack (to be retrieved so that the program can continue where it left off once the interrupt event is over), and the address of the interrupt-handler is placed in the program counter register. Thus, on the next execution cycle the central processing unit will execute the first instruction in the interrupt-handler, and so on.

Events that could cause interrupts include changes of state in peripheral devices (a printer running out of paper, or completion of a disc-to-memory data transfer), an execution error of some sort (such as trying to access a non-existent address), a priority interrupt in a multi-tasking system (where a process of higher priority has become available to use the CPU), a manual interrupt (where the human operator overrides the current program), or a timed interrupt (where a process has been allocated a fixed time slice, and that time is up).

The interrupt-handler will determine the nature of the interrupt by working through a list of the possible causes, and then take appropriate action by transferring control of the execution cycle to the relevant section of the operating system (using an address from a list of interrupt 'vectors'). That action could be as simple as displaying a message ('printer out of paper'), it could involve allocating a new task to a peripheral, or it could involve terminating the current process permanently (rather than simply suspending it) and then displaying an error message. Once the interrupt has been dealt with, the suspended program will be reactivated to resume processing (unless it has been terminated or superseded by a higher priority process).

If two interrupt events occur together, then the order in which the list of causes is checked determines the order in which they are dealt with. Crucial events leading to loss of data (impending power failure), appear in front of events affecting the efficiency of the CPU (higher priority processes), that appear in front of events carrying no risk at all (printer out of paper).

*see also...*

*Operating system; Stack*

# *Legislation*

As IT becomes more widely used for the storage of information, and as computing technologies have become networkable and therefore accessible from remote locations, the perceived need for governments to legislate in its use has grown. Indeed, IT has long brought up issues of power and control, but until recently, was a curiously legislation-free zone, with governments either not recognizing IT as important enough to merit legal attention, or feeling unable to act. In a practical sense, since much IT use takes 'place' over the wires of global networks, it lacks a physical place where laws could apply. Also, from a philosophical viewpoint, IT users have traditionally resented any attempts from outside agencies to regulate or control their activities.

Yet many governments *have* brought in legislation to attempt to regulate IT use, such as data protection acts to address personal privacy with regard to information held about individuals in databases and files. The UK Data Protection Acts of 1984 and 1998 require personal data held on computer systems to be securely processed, held for specific purposes and only to be stored for as long as is strictly necessary. In addition, they allow people some right of access to records held about them. However, the fact remains that in practice such legislation is difficult to enforce.

More controversial have been some governments' attempts to curtail 'undesirable' IT use. The UK's 'Computer Misuse Act', for example, made it a criminal offence to attempt to access or modify computer-held data without authority – covering both cracking computer systems and the distribution of viruses. More controversial still is legislation aiming to increase governments' rights to monitor an individual's IT use – including the surveillance of on-line activity, such as computer mediated communication. In the UK, recent legislation has been passed to allow the police to intercept e-mail and other forms of electronic communication.

Legislation of IT use will increase in prominence as the level of people's IT increases. Much criticism has focused on issues of civil liberties – warning against an Orwellian 'Big Brother' scenario and the emergence of a surveillance state.

*see also...*

**Super-Panopticon**

# Linux

Linux is an operating system for computers, based on the 30-year-old UNIX operating system, that is used mainly by programmers and 'expert' users. Since its initial development in 1991 by a Finnish student, Linus Torvalds, Linux has quickly developed as the operating system of choice for many computer programmers and enthusiasts. Now Linux boasts over ten million users and a large proportion of the world wide web is run on Linux code. The significance of Linux is that, unlike other operating systems such as the dominant Microsoft Windows, it is freely available to anyone who wants to use it. Moreover, programmers are able to improve and develop new versions that are then, in turn, distributed freely to anyone who wants them. The success of this principle, known as 'open source', has caught many computer companies by surprise and is seen as an example of the 'people power' that computing was originally based on in the 1970s and 1980s. Linux is seen as posing a significant challenge to the commercial dominance of software companies such as Microsoft.

Technically, Linux has proved successful because of its simple design. The main operating code is known as the kernel, which is a small but powerful modular operating system able to load different functions when they are needed and then free up the computer's memory when they have been finished with. This is unlike other operating systems, such as Microsoft Windows, that load everything onto the computer, whether it is needed or not, for all of the time it is being used – thus slowing down the computer and wasting memory. Because of this design, Linux is considered by computer programmers to be very fast, stable and flexible – hence its enduring popularity.

Yet the real success of Linux lies in the 'open source' principle where the source code of computer programs should be made freely available to other computer users. Linux is therefore now distributed under a 'copyleft' (as opposed to copyright) stipulation that any modified version that is produced must be freely distributed. In practice, this has proved highly successful, with powerful and improved versions of Linux code being developed and users able to choose between the latest 'stable' release and the latest 'experimental' release.

*see also...*

*Hacker; Operating system*

# *Logical error*

A logical error is a mistake in the algorithm used in a program. The program does not do what is required and the blame for this lies with the programmer. A logical error is like an incorrect but comprehensible verbal instruction. If I want you to move to your right and I ask you to 'Wxre1#4', you will be unable to comply because you will not understand what I am saying (a syntax error). If I ask you to 'move to your left', you will do the opposite to what was intended. In the first case, you will realize that there has been an error and let me know. In the second case, the instruction is perfectly valid, but it is also wrong. This is a 'logical' error, and is more dangerous as it is harder to spot.

Such logical errors are easy to make, and one reason for this is that we become used to being somewhat imprecise in conversation. This often goes unnoticed because our listeners make intelligent assumptions. Computers are unable to do this. A simple example might involve the logical operation OR. In English, the word 'or' is used in two very different ways. If someone asked you whether you wished to go to France or Australia on your holiday, you would hardly imagine that you could do both, yet this is what OR means in logic.

Imagine that you wished a new program to continue executing in a loop, until either or both of two variables (x, y) reach the value zero, then the coding might look like this:

REPEAT … UNTIL x=0 OR y=0

If you chose to express the same thing negatively by continuing the loop while neither variable had the value zero, you might code it like this:

DOWHILE x<>0 OR y<>0 … ENDDO

This version would be incorrect. It would appear to work sometimes and this could make the error hard to spot. Therefore, programs need to be thoroughly tested before being put to real use. Removal of logical errors and running tests cannot prove that there are no more errors. Our default assumption must be that any complex piece of software contains some logical errors as yet unrevealed. This is one reason why some observers say that the US 'Star Wars' missile defence system can never be reliable.

*see also...*

*Algorithm; Program*

# Lovelace, Ada

Augusta Ada Byron (1815–52), later known as Ada, Countess of Lovelace, is one of the most significant and interesting figures in the history of computing. Ada referred to herself as an 'analyst and metaphysician' and is now seen as an important figure in the development of modern-day computers and computer programming.

The estranged daughter of the Romantic poet Lord Byron, Ada was brought up by her mother to be as unlike her father as possible, and was encouraged to study science and mathematics. When she was only 17 years old, Ada met the inventor of the Difference Engine, Charles Babbage. The Difference Engine was an elaborate calculating machine, but even before it was finished Babbage was already working on plans for a second machine – the Analytical Engine. The meeting between Babbage and Byron in 1833 is now seen as the birth of scientific computing, as well as a lifelong friendship and working relationship between them.

Babbage asked Byron to assist him in the development of the Analytical Engine – writing extensive notes on the use and possible applications of the machine. Her published notes in 1843 included a set of instructions for programming the Analytical Engine using Bernoulli numbers – now regarded as the first 'computer program'. Within these notes she also speculated on the use of the machine for the 'developping [*sic*] and tabulating of any function whatever' as well as foreseeing the application of such machines for graphics, musical composition and artificial intelligence.

In her work with Babbage, Ada was one of the pioneers of modern-day computing, particularly software development. She foresaw the vast potential of the Analytical Engine, although her work was not widely recognized until the second half of the twentieth century. Recently, she has been rediscovered as a figurehead for the role of women in computing and her pioneering work was acknowledged when the US Department of Defence named a software language 'Ada' in her honour in 1979.

see also...

*Babbage, Charles; Programming language*

# *Luddism*

Resistance to technology and technological change has a long history – reflected in the enduring use of the term 'Luddite' to describe anyone who is distrustful or fearful of changes brought about by new technology. The Luddites were groups of disaffected textile workers in England who, between 1811 and 1817, set about breaking machines that were beginning to be used in textile factories as a mechanical means of cutting cloth – a task which had previously been the preserve of specialized workers.

The case of the Luddites provides an interesting example of how any interpretation of technology and society is not straightforward. Two centuries on, a conventional perspective remains that the Luddites were ignorantly and irrationally attacking machines that were capable of increased productivity and ultimately advancing human progress. This view led to the disparaging connotations that the term 'Luddite' holds to this day. However, the idea that it was the inherent qualities of the machines that prompted the Luddites is dubious. The machines in question had been used for a few years before 1811 and, in any event, the incidence of actual machine breaking was relatively slight. Instead, it can be argued that the Luddites were not opposed to the technology *per se*, rather that they were attacking the machines as a symbolic metaphor for a wider struggle against the emerging capitalism of the industrial revolution, as well as the debilitating effects of the recent Napoleonic war, the growth of factories and the effects of recent poor harvests.

Despite this misunderstanding of Luddism, the term has now been claimed by new groups of people wanting to raise moral and ethical concerns against the excesses of modern technology and the extent that it threatens humanity. These self-styled 'neo-Luddites' are critiquing the rise of technological development. Despite a lack of uniformity among its members, neo-Luddism is generally seen to oppose the view that technological development is inevitable and socially beneficial. Neo-Luddites would instead point towards technology's role in the perpetuation of capitalist society, as well as highlighting the negative impacts of new technology on humans, natural systems and the environment.

*see also...*

*Technological utopianism*

# Memory

The memory is where the computer stores the instructions for any programs being run (or 'executed') and any data in immediate use by those programs. Memory is divided into locations or registers, which contain a series of binary digits equal to the 'word' length of the computer. Each location could be storing a number, character or machine instruction. There is nothing in the pattern of binary digits to distinguish between these alternatives, since the same sequence of bits can mean different things in different contexts.

Reading the contents of a location involves the central processing unit (CPU) in passing an address along the address bus to the memory address register (MAR). There, the address is converted into the x, y co-ordinates needed to specify one memory location. The binary number within this unique location is passed to the memory data register (MDR), and then along the data bus to any other register in the CPU (such as the accumulator), as required. Writing new contents to a location involves similar steps, with the addition that a write-control signal is sent to memory, and the binary number representing the new contents is passed along the data bus to the MDR at the same time as the address is sent to the MAR.

Memory that operates in this way is known as Random Access Memory (RAM), since it can be accessed in any order, and the speed with which each location can be read does not depend on the size of the memory or the position of last location accessed (unlike direct or serial access memories). This form of memory is generally volatile, meaning that the computer requires power to keep refreshing it. In the absence of power, the RAM contents are lost (which is why you need to save your files on disc). Some parts of the memory contain information that is too important to be lost in this way. An example of such information is the bootstrap program, executed at start-up, that is the minimal number of instructions needed to allow the operating system software to be read from a storage device. Such information is stored in a type of RAM that is not volatile, does not allow over-writing of its contents, and is generally referred to as Read Only Memory (or ROM).

*see also...*

*Central processing unit; Memory address; Storage device*

# Memory address

An address is a number used to designate the location of a piece of data in a computer's memory. Main memory inside a computer is divided into separate locations, or registers. Each register stores a sequence of binary digits known as one 'word' and each register has a uniquely numbered address. The address is used whenever a word is read from, or written to, that register.

Most machine instructions have two parts to their syntax – the operation and operand. The operation is the action to be carried out (such as add, move, copy) and the operand specifies the data to be acted on. This operand is usually an address. For example, 'Add 1307' might instruct a machine to add the binary digits in the address numbered 1307, to the binary digits stored in another location (usually the accumulator register). In this case, the operation ('Add') has two operands. One is referred to directly ('1307') and the other is implied (the accumulator register).

The operand, or address part, of a machine instruction can be used in several different ways, known as addressing modes. Direct and implied addressing are two of these. Another mode of address is 'immediate' which is not really an address at all but a literal value. For example, the instruction 'Add immediate 1307' means add the number 1307 to the accumulator. Indirect addressing involves using the value in the location specified in the operand as the actual address. So, the instruction 'Add indirect 1307' would mean add the value in the location whose address is in location 1307 to the accumulator. If location 1307 contains the number 245, the instruction adds the contents of location 245 to the accumulator. The chief advantage of this is that the address in 1307 is variable.

Another mode of addressing is 'relative', in which the operand is added to a base number to create the actual address used. By changing the base number, it is possible to move the program and still run it from anywhere in the memory. When there is more than one program running at once (multi-tasking), as there usually is in a modern computer, this flexibility is very useful.

see also...

Arithmetic-logic unit; Central processing unit; Memory

# Microsoft

**A**s the world's leading software company, Microsoft Corporation is synonymous with computer software for many people. Around 85 per cent of all personal computers are currently sold with the Microsoft Windows operating system. As such, Microsoft is an example of the spectacular growth of computing as a commercial activity in recent times, and of how IT has moved from a hobbyist activity to a multinational corporate concern.

Microsoft was set up in 1975 by two school friends – Bill Gates and Paul Allen. The pair wrote a version of the BASIC computer programming language and managed to sell it to a company that was producing a computer called the Altair. After this initial success, Gates sold his Microsoft Disc Operating System (MS-DOS) to the IBM company in 1980. Gates cleverly did not grant IBM an exclusive licence, which meant that other companies soon began to use MS-DOS for their computers as well. The dominance of Microsoft was cemented in 1985 with the release of their Windows graphical user interface. Windows and its subsequent upgrades quickly established Microsoft as the world's most visible computer company, and Gates and Allen as two of the most high profile IT entrepreneurs.

As the world's most successful software company, Microsoft is also one of the most controversial. Critics argue that its success has been based less on innovation and more on ruthlessly adapting pre-existing ideas such as the development of Windows as a graphical user interface and the Explorer web browser. Yet in both cases Microsoft has been incredibly successful in eventually dominating the marketplace and making its software synonymous with computing in that area.

In doing so, Microsoft has successfully combined two vital traits in the IT industry – relentless technological *and* commercial ambition, although its market dominance was recently challenged by the US Department of Justice which investigated the company to see if it was abusing its monopoly power.

## see also...
*Apple; IBM; Software*

# Moore's Law

**M**oore's Law was first suggested by Gordon Moore, the co-founder of the Intel microchip manufacturing company. In 1965, Moore made the observation in a speech that the number of transistors able to be put on a microchip appeared to be doubling every 18 to 24 months. Moore's remark neatly illustrated the exponential rise of computing power at a time when it was doubling approximately every two years. Nevertheless, the notion of Moore's Law has endured long since it was originally coined. This 'ball-park' estimation of technological advance has since been popularly refined to now state that the number of transistors able to be put on a microchip doubles every year and a half whilst the price remains constant. In other words, computing power is quadrupling every three years – so that the computer that you buy today is four times more powerful than the one that you could have purchased three years ago for the same price.

The most striking feature of Moore's Law is that it has remained remarkably accurate – a major achievement given the notorious unpredictability of information technology development. Indeed, from the beginning of the 1970s to the end of the 1990s, the number of transistors (or their equivalent) on a microchip increased more than 3,500 times, with present-day microchips now featuring around 8 million transistors. Because of its apparent accuracy, Moore's original observation was quickly taken up by the IT industry and has since formed the basis for many official performance forecasts and targets set by firms. Most experts, including Gordon Moore himself, predict that Moore's Law will remain accurate for at least another two decades.

> **see also...**
> *Futurology*

# Multimedia

Like many terms in IT, multimedia has come to mean many things to different people and, in some instances, is used merely to denote any modern information and communications technology application – tending to imply sophisticated and modern-day new media technology. However, in a strict sense, multimedia refers to the integrated presentation of data, text, graphics, video and sound on a computer or other digital environment. Most common forms of multimedia are the world wide web, digital television and computer based CD-ROMs, all offering a blend of sound, images and text. The fundamental principle behind multimedia is digitization – the conversion of images and sounds to numbers that can then be processed and manipulated by computers before being re-presented as images and sounds on screen. Although multimedia was long seen as a significant IT application, it was not until the 1990s that its use became widespread as PCs were developed that were capable of handling video and sound.

Multimedia facilitates the convergence of many different IT applications onto single technologies. Computers are now capable of playing feature films, music CDs and radio stations. Similarly, digital television and mobile telephones are capable of providing access to the world wide web and e-mail. In theory, multimedia will open up the use of many different IT applications to users via one point of access. The idea of multimedia is also an interesting example of a computing idea waiting to happen. Indeed, multimedia was touted as a revolutionary application long before even the most powerful computers were capable of running such applications. Multimedia is now seen as a slightly jaded and embarrassing label by many IT enthusiasts. The term was commonly used throughout the 1960s and 1970s to describe the use of film or slide strips with accompanying audio soundtracks played on a tape recorder. Thus, at the beginning of the 1980s, the computer pioneer Ted Nelson described it as a 'resurrected and irrelevant' term for the 'brave new world' of IT. Nevertheless, its use has persisted in describing some modern-day IT applications.

*see also...*

*Hypertext*

64

# Multi-tasking

This term denotes a range of related situations. The common theme is that more than one process or task is apparently being executed by a computer simultaneously. In fact, this concept can be divided into parallel or concurrent processing, where the system has more than one processor, and multi-programming/multi-user systems that merely give the appearance of doing more than one thing at once.

Parallel processing is rare, and usually reserved for tasks of great urgency which can be broken down into component parts to be executed in parallel. Techniques such as critical path analysis are used to determine which parts of the job are dependent on a precise sequence, and which parts can be 'sub-contracted' to another processor. More common is a form of distributed processing where the main central processing unit (CPU) is assisted by one or more distributed processors. The extra processing facilities are often for specialist tasks, such as memory to peripheral transfer, that can be conducted at the same time as more general processing. Networks operate in a similar way, where each terminal is actually a computer in its own right, able to conduct a limited amount of processing 'off-line' from the network CPU.

Multi-tasking also refers to a situation in which several jobs are available for processing but only one is being processed at once. One way of doing this is to give each task or user a time-slice in sequence. If a computer has three users at one time, it can simply divide its time between the three. The CPU executes instructions from one user until a timed interrupt passes control to the next user and so on. If the computer is fast enough none of the other users will be aware that they are not the only ones that the computer is dealing with. As the number of users increases, so the length or frequency of their time-slices will decrease and the system will appear to slow down. Rather than using simple timed interrupts, a more efficient method is to combine these with a polling system. At each timed interrupt, the operating system determines the nature of activities of the next user. If these involve waiting, for a peripheral transfer, for example, then control is passed to the next user in sequence. Thus, execution cycles are not wasted on users who do not need them at that instant.

## see also...

On/off-line; Operating system

# National information infrastructure

One of the key political issues of the moment is whether individual nations retain the ability to exert control over their destinies in the face of the information technology-based 'global' economy. Many commentators have been keen to predict the 'death' of the individual country in the borderless information age, as multinational corporations play a more powerful role in shaping the twenty-first century.

In response to these global changes, many 'developed' countries such as those in North America, Europe and East Asia have been developing policy initiatives aimed at increasing the use of IT among their populations for economic and social purposes – a trend referred to as creating 'national information infrastructures' (NII). In an organizational sense, a national information infrastructure encompasses all computerized networks, applications and services that citizens in a country can use to access, create, disseminate and utilize digital information. In practice, therefore, NII policy programmes have tended to involve the diffusion of technologies as diverse as mobile telephony, digital broadcasting, the Internet and other multimedia, in both the private and public sectors.

Perhaps the best example of NII policymaking can be seen in the sustained efforts of the Clinton/Gore administration throughout the 1990s, to create a 'US National Information Infrastructure' based around an information and communications network connecting homes, businesses and public institutions to the 'information superhighway'. In East Asia, many countries have pursued explicit NII policy agendas vigorously during the 1990s. Malaysia's NII policy has taken the form of 'Vision 2020', a 25-year plan to create a 'technologically driven nation' with the building of an 'intelligent city' (Cyberjaya), new 'cyberlaws' to encourage electronic commerce, coupled with a high capacity national IT infrastructure.

National information infrastructures are a practical manifestation of the idea that individual countries can still shape their own destinies in this IT-dominated age. Their significance will be seen in the success that such policies will have (or not have) over the next two decades.

see also...

*Information superhighway*

# *Network*

A network is a series of points (also known as nodes) connected together by communication paths. In practice, the concept of linking computers (or terminals) together in networks to permit the transfer of data (and the distribution of processing power) has been at the heart of developments in information technology over the last 20 years. The development of networking technologies has extended the capabilities and potential of individual 'stand-alone' computers and facilitated a convergence of information technologies and telecommunications technologies. Now, through the networking of computers together on a local basis, such as in a school or office or in the global network of the Internet, it is a crucial aspect of IT.

Computer networks can be characterized in different ways: the types of physical links (e.g. fibreoptic); the nature of the connections (e.g. dial-up); or the geometric arrangement of the nodes and pathways (e.g. a star or ring arrangement). The spatial distance between nodes is also used as a type of classification, distinguishing between 'local-area networks' (usually denoting networks of closely situated computers such as in a school), 'metropolitan-area networks' and other far more dispersed 'wide-area networks'.

Networks are important as they allow the simultaneous exchange of data by many individual users who can be geographically and temporally dispersed. At one level, a network allows all of its users to access computer software and other forms of data at the same time. This means that many users can gain access to the same product without it having to be distributed to them on an individual basis, making the distribution of software and data a far less time-consuming and costly process. Networks are also invaluable as they allow users to have access to each other – thus facilitating computer mediated communication. The creation of global networks by allowing the connection of many different networks together (as in the case of the Internet) has further extended the utility and flexibility of networks. Indeed, many commentators have pointed towards the networking logic of information technologies as permeating into social systems of organizations around the world and thus creating a 'network society'.

*see also...*

*Internet; Network society*

# Network society

The notion of a 'network society' is an attempt by the academic, Manuel Castells, to expand upon the idea of the information society. For Castells, one of the key features of the information society is the 'networking logic' of its basic structure. In other words, the dominant functions and processes in the information society are increasingly organized around networks rather than physical boundaries. Castells sees the rising importance of networks in society as being brought about by developments in IT and the restructuring of capitalism and nation states in the 1980s, as well as the rise of social movements such as feminism and ecologism. Castells also argues that a reliance on networks has led to the redefinition of time and space in contemporary life – suggesting, for example, that the network society is organized around the 'space of flows' (i.e. the movement of information or money) rather than the space of places (i.e. their original location).

This idea of the network society can be best seen in contemporary patterns of economic activity that depend ultimately on the dynamics of the 'global' economy rather than any national influence. It can also be seen in the 'network enterprise' of modern trans-national corporations, the networking of labour in the form of 'flexi-workers', as well as in 'global' social movements such as the ongoing anti-capitalist campaigns. While networking has existed as a form of social organization in other times, Castells stresses that it is the widespread emergence of information technology that has made it a dominant feature of life in the early twenty-first century. Thus, it is the global transmission of information that is at the heart of countries' prosperity and competitiveness in the 'information society'.

Although based on extensive empirical examination of global trends over the last two decades, Castells's notion of the network society has been attacked by critics for its over-simplification and a tendency towards technological determinism. Nevertheless, it can be seen as a more refined and detailed 'fleshing out' of the information society thesis of the 1970s and, therefore, a useful metaphor for the impact of ICT on contemporary life in 'developed' societies.

> ### see also...
> Information society; Network

# On/off-line

On-line parts of a computer system are connected to the central processing unit (CPU) and usable by it. Off-line parts of a computer system are either not connected to the CPU or are otherwise not usable at that present time. The terms usually refer to peripheral devices or to programs and procedures, but off-line can also refer to events disconnected from a computer, such as human activities like reading, carrying or editing. Typical off-line processes include the preparation of data for input to a system or editing a computer printout with a pen before making changes on screen. Typical on-line processes include loading a file or playing an interactive game.

Of course, the clear distinction between on- and off-line is commonly weakened in the use of a networked computer. Quite often the terminal connected to the network is itself a personal computer (PC), but the connection is to a more powerful mainframe computer. In this example, the user may begin a session on-line to their own PC but off-line as far as the network is concerned. Their first action may be to log-on to the network computer thereby becoming on-line to that as well. Thereafter, some actions will be on-line to the mainframe (running

a new networked program, for example) and some will be off-line (editing on the word processing package from their PC, for example).

Where such a system is multi-tasking or multi-programming, a number of different programs may be available to run at any time. Of these, only one can be executed at a time (unless there is a multiple processor). The one being executed is therefore on-line, and the others are temporarily off-line. In a multi-user system, where one processor is apparently being used simultaneously by a number of users, it is also the case that only one at a time can be on-line. A simple method of organizing this is for the operating system to allocate each user a time-slice, or period, when they have control of the processor, until a timed interrupt moves control to the next user, and the previous user goes off-line. Since the processor is so fast in comparison to most tasks undertaken by users in real-time (such as typing), this slicing goes on without users generally being aware of it.

*see also...*

Computer; Multi-tasking; Operating system

# Operating system

This is a piece of systems software which isolates a computer user from the actual machine they are using. The operating system (OS) is a program running intermittently whenever the machine is switched on, which creates an illusory ('virtual') machine that the user interacts with. A computer is a very complex set of electronic circuits, but since it is programmable, the designer has written systems software (programs) to present the user with a simplified and much easier to use system. Thus, using a computer actually involves interacting with a pre-written program. Although the operating system is a program, and therefore 'software', it is an integral part of a computer, and therefore closely linked to the 'hardware'. Programs like operating systems are sometimes referred to as 'firmware'.

The same hardware can run different operating systems, and will therefore appear to be a different machine. This is the basis of emulation, where one machine mimics the hardware of another, allowing the transfer of files and even programs between them. Similarly, different hardware can also run the same operating system, and therefore appear to be more alike than they really are. Well-known operating systems are MS-DOS and UNIX.

The role of the operating system is to manage the memory by allocating each process a segment of memory, to control the peripherals allowing them to transfer or store data semi-autonomously from the central processing unit (CPU), and to schedule tasks for execution by the CPU. Programs, processes and other tasks are usually executed by the CPU in priority order and it is the role of the operating system to decide which task takes precedence next and to handle the interruption of the current process when a higher priority task arises. The priority of each task is usually based on a mixture of urgency (i.e. what needs to be done first) and efficiency (i.e. which order allows the greatest throughput).

The human operator can be defined as the hands and legs of the operating system, carrying out tasks that the operating system cannot. These include removing discs from drives, and replacing paper in printers. In small personal systems, the user is also the operator. In larger systems, operating is a specialist task for those in the machine room during operation.

*see also...*

*Interrupt; Linux; Virtual machine*

70

# *Optical fibre*

An optical fibre is a wire made of transparent fibre, used to transport information between sites using optical (light) signals. Transmission is extremely fast compared to its predecessors, such as electrical and coaxial cabling, and also allows more cabling to fit into a certain space. The signal also degrades less over distance, making it more attractive as an alternative to broadcast systems that use radio and television transmitters as well. This means it is likely to be the method of choice for the near future, used for digital television as well as the Internet and related computer applications. It makes the transmission of sound and pictures via cable over long distances routine, for perhaps the first time.

Since the devices actually connected via these optical fibres do not usually process optical signals, converters are needed at each end – one to convert electronic signals into light energy, and another for the reverse conversion (compare the role of a modem or **mo**dulator/**dem**odulator for telephone lines).

Computer storage devices have been created involving optical storage principles, such as optical discs or tapes, rather than the more usual magnetic-based ones. Optical devices are still significantly more expensive, but have a higher volume capacity (technically: 'packing density') than magnetic discs. They are also more prone to random error during storage and recovery of information than magnetic devices (although, of course, less troubled by magnetic radiation). This makes them more suitable for the storage and transmission of high-density data with considerable redundancy (so that a few minor errors will not invalidate the whole dataset). Such applications are provided by the storage and transmission of sound, and especially of graphics, where the alteration of the odd picture element, or pixel, does not make the picture unrecognizable.

*see also...*

*Baud; Corruption*

# Output device

A peripheral is a device within a computer system that is outside of, but often connected to, the central processing unit. These are commonly divided into storage devices (such as discs), input devices (such as a keyboard) and output devices (such as a screen). An output device is a part of the hardware in any system. It is used to transfer data from a computer system to the external world.

Examples of output devices include the visual display unit (VDU) or monitor, printer and sound generator. On the simplest forms of screen display, each character appears in a standard size so that the screen has a pre-determined number of character spaces (such as 160 wide and 40 high). Each character's ASCII code is converted for display from one byte to a pattern of bytes which themselves determine what appears on the screen. For example, the letter 'H' is 72 (or 01001010 in binary), but its display code might be 102, 102, 126, 126, 102, and 102, or in binary:

$$01100110$$
$$01100110$$
$$01111110$$
$$01111110$$
$$01100110$$
$$01100110$$

If a 1 leads to a spot of light in one small part of the screen (pixel), and 0 leads to no spot, then this will look like the letter 'H'. Similar principles were used with the old-fashioned 'dot-matrix' printer. Modern-day computers use a more flexible approach, allowing each pixel to be addressed individually, not needing pre-determined character positions on the screen, allowing different fonts, sizes and free-form graphics. Instead of using one bit for each pixel (as in monochrome displays), several bits can be used to determine the presence or absence of the spot, and also its colour and intensity. Naturally, this flexibility requires considerably more memory.

Printing is generally so slow in comparison to other system activities that it is often conducted off-line using a technique called spooling (short for simultaneous peripheral operation on-line). Instead of using the buffer arrangement (see Input device), the entire file to be printed is saved quickly to a temporary backing store to be printed later, releasing the processor to continue with other tasks.

## see also...

ASCII; Central processing unit

# *Pervasive computing*

The idea of pervasive computing (or ubiquitous computing as it is also referred to) is one of the current obsessions of the IT industry and is seen as the 'next big thing' by many hardware and software manufacturers. Pervasive computing is the notion that information technology is moving beyond fixed, obtrusive 'stand-alone' devices (such as the personal computer), towards smaller connected computing devices that are embedded into our environment. Pervasive computing stems from the convergence and miniaturization of information technologies, as well as the growth of networking, wireless technology, voice recognition and artificial intelligence software. The goal of pervasive computing is, therefore, to create a constantly available technology system that is embedded into the environment: completely connected, intuitive to use and an integral but unobtrusive part of everyday life.

On one level, the idea of pervasive computing is an accurate description of technologies that are already beginning to be used in society. The use of the personal computer, Internet and mobile telephone into handheld wireless computing devices is growing in popularity, allowing users constant connectivity to information and communication regardless of time or location. As a way of describing wireless and mobile computing, the idea of pervasive computing is an accurate indication of where IT could be heading over the next decade.

On another level, however, the idea of pervasive computing is far more radical. In its extreme definition, pervasive computing is the idea that all man-made products (and even some natural products) will have some computing embedded in them. Technologists talk of 'smart devices' that can plug into 'intelligent networks' – envisaging all aspects of life being seamlessly run through a connected network of computing devices. Pervasive computing is also the idea that everything (cars, tools, household appliances, clothing, etc.), will have embedded computers connecting them to a network of other devices. This is seen as leading to 'smart homes' and 'smart offices' and to a society fundamentally entwined with information technology.

> **see also...**
> *Artificial intelligence; Futurology*

# Programming language

Computers need instructions in order to perform specific tasks – supplied in the form of programs. Programs are expressed in a programming language, the simplest of which is a machine code with a limited set of machine instructions. This set of instructions differs between different types of processor. Programs expressed in machine code are not transferable between, and will not run on, different kinds of computers. In addition, machine code is expressed as a series of binary numbers, making it hard for humans to work with. To overcome this weakness, most computers also have an 'assembly' code that is a form of the machine code but with the instructions expressed as mnemonics (easy to remember terms) and the operands expressed in symbols and base ten numbers.

An assembly instruction might be 'ADD #43', meaning add the value 43 to the number in the accumulator. Since computers only execute machine code, this instruction would need to be converted into its machine code equivalent before execution – a process known as assembly. If the assembly process encounters an instruction that it cannot translate, it is reported as a syntax error. Since a syntax error means that the machine code is incomplete, the program will not be executable until the syntax error is corrected.

Both machine code and assembly code are seen as 'low-level' languages, far removed from a natural language such as English. By comparison, high-level programming languages offer many advantages. Programs in high-level languages are generally portable between machines. Each instruction in a high-level language would be translated (via a more complex process than assembly) into many machine instructions. Each high-level instruction does more work than one machine instruction, so it is easier to write longer complex programs.

These languages can be made more like natural language, understandable by human programmers, and tailored to suit programming particular applications. Of the long-established languages, FORTRAN (formula translator) was designed for use by mathematicians and scientists, COBOL (common business oriented language) was designed for use in standard commercial applications. Other popular languages include BASIC, 'C', Pascal, and Logo.

## see also...
Syntax; Translation

74

# Robotics

The word 'robot' was coined by the Czech playwright Karel Capek in the 1920s, deriving from the Czech word for forced labour. A key theme in Capek's play *R.U.R.* (Rossum's Universal Robots) was the dehumanization of humans in a technological civilization populated by robots. The term 'robot' was subsequently adopted by engineers and computer scientists to refer to mechanical devices that move and react to sensory input – often performing functions normally ascribed to humans. The word 'robotics', referring to the study and use of robots, was then coined by the writer Isaac Asimov in 1942. Asimov also proposed three 'Laws of Robotics', later also adding a prefacing 'zeroth' law:

**0** A robot may not injure humanity or, through inaction, allow humanity to come to harm.
**1** A robot may not injure a human being or, through inaction, allow a human being to come to harm, unless this would violate a higher order law.
**2** A robot must obey orders given it by human beings, except where such orders would conflict with a higher order law.
**3** A robot must protect its own existence as long as such protection does not conflict with a higher order law.

Although robotics attracted a lot of attention throughout the twentieth century, the practical application of robots has proved limited. The first industrial modern robots were developed during the late 1950s, culminating in the industrial arms designed for use in factories. During the 1950s, the image of the robot as some sort of mechanical human was a popular device in books, television and films – acting as a symbol of technological progress and life 'in the future'. However, from the 1960s and 1970s, the general use of robots has been constrained to industrial settings, where they perform high-precision jobs such as welding and riveting.

Although great advances have been made in the field of robotics during the last decade, robots have so far failed to live up to early expectations. Thus, it is mainly the theoretical implications and technical challenges that make robotics a key idea in IT.

## see also...
*Artificial intelligence*

# Simulation

A simulation is the process of imitating the behaviour of some real or imagined system through a mathematical model. This model can then be used to see how a system operates and, by altering variables in the system, make predictions about how the system may change under different circumstances and conditions. As essentially very powerful manipulators of numbers, computers are ideally suited to running simulations. Particular examples include computer-generated simulations of large systems such as economic forecasts, weather patterns, biological and chemical processes. However, simulations of smaller systems such as aeroplanes, cars and other machines are also widely used. Their main advantages are the speed with which the 'future' can be played out, the low cost, and the lack of risk and ethical considerations.

Computer simulations can either be 'discrete event' simulations or 'continuous' simulations. A continuous simulation views changes to a system as occurring gradually and simultaneously over time and, therefore, simply models the progress of these gradual changes together. In this way, a dynamic model is produced of the process being simulated with the computer producing a continuous history of the process based on a set of initial conditions. A discrete event simulation, on the other hand, treats each significant change to the system as a distinct event that must be modelled separately. Whereas a discrete event simulation may be easier to control and alter individual variables, it could be seen as less of a 'real-life' model than a continuous simulation.

Simulations can be based around the creation of a mathematical model of the system that the computer can manipulate by changing variables and making mathematical predictions as to how the system will change. In theory, therefore, any system or phenomena that can be modelled around mathematical data and formulae can be simulated. However, the conversion of real-life events and processes into numbers is problematic and can never be totally accurate.

Many real-life phenomena such as weather systems or diseases are subject to a huge number of influences – all of which cannot be included in the simulation. The accuracy of all simulations, therefore, relies on the programmers correctly determining the most important factors to include in the model.

# *Sinclair, Clive*

live Sinclair (1940–) is a British innovator and businessman who can be credited with introducing computers into millions of UK homes during the 1980s. A generation of Britons grew up with Sinclair home computers – transforming computing from an specialized hobby into a mainstream leisure activity.

Sinclair had been a successful inventor and entrepreneur throughout the 1960s and 1970s, gaining a reputation for his pioneering pocket calculators and digital wristwatches. As a businessman, Sinclair had also been tremendously successful, producing electronic goods in bulk and selling them at low prices. By the end of the 1970s, the sales of his MX14 microcomputer kit persuaded Sinclair that computing was worthy of mass marketing to the general public. By 1980, he had launched the Sinclair ZX80 at a retail price of only £99.95 (designed for use with a home TV screen). The introduction of such a cheap personal computer was highly significant. At the time, computers were expensive and unwieldy, but Sinclair saw the opportunity to produce affordable machines for 'the common man'. Despite its primitive capabilities, the ZX80 was a considerable success, prompting the launch of the improved ZX81 a year later.

Finally, in 1982, the ZX Spectrum was launched – a more powerful computer, capable of colour graphics, limited sound, and able to run a wide range of computer games. With sales quickly running into millions, the ZX Spectrum played a part in establishing the home computer as a mainstream household good.

Sinclair's success had a profound effect on the way that the UK public treated IT. Although his computers were not that technically advanced, Sinclair was seen as leading Britain's entry into the 'information age' and was knighted in 1983. Sinclair was one of the first companies to advertise home computers widely and market them in high street shops as well as in specialist electrical stores. A range of companies emerged to produce software and peripherals for Sinclair machines and home computing was soon established as a highly lucrative market. Unfortunately, Sinclair's success was later halted by a commercially disastrous attempt to produce a plastic, battery-powered three-wheeled vehicle – the Sinclair C5. Although he has since continued to design electronic goods, Sinclair will undoubtedly be best remembered as the father of home computing in the UK.

# Software

Software is a general term for those elements of a computer system that are not physical. It generally refers to programs executed by the computer, rather than the computer itself. A program is a series of instructions for a computer to carry out a particular task. Most commonly, the term refers to a procedural program, which specifies each step leading to the desired result. These steps would be based on an algorithm. If you can imagine everything that a computer does in terms of procedural steps, it is easier to understand that generally a computer cannot do anything that a person could not do. It can do things repetitively, accurately and quickly.

At the most basic level, a program would be in machine-coded form, using a binary number (or code) for each instruction and its parameters. For convenience, these numbers can be written and communicated in base 16 (hexadecimal) where each hex digit represents four binary digits (conventionally using the letters A to F to represent 1010 to 1111). Most programs are, however, written in a higher-level symbolic form, and some are written using general problem

solving modules, meaning that the precise steps necessary for a solution are implicit rather than explicit.

Software is generally categorized into two genres. Applications software is a program, or a set of programs, used to carry out a computer application such as running a company payroll. An application program sets out to meet the end-user's needs directly. Applications software is therefore more often tailored to specific users' requirements, and has to be engineered from scratch or modified accordingly. This can be contrasted with systems software, such as the operating system, which is concerned with the operation of the computer system and translation programs such as assemblers, compilers, interpreters and program generators. It is also distinct from content-free software, such as word processors, that are not system-based. They are for the benefit of the user, but have no specific application.

## see also...

*Algorithm; Binary; Programming language; Software engineering*

# Software engineering

The term software engineering implies a change of practice. Whereas programmers might have originally been seen as individuals who were successful if they produced a working solution, this is no longer deemed sufficient. Software engineering covers not only the technical elements of programming software applications, but also managing, scheduling and budgeting the development of software. Software is now usually produced in teams, and programmers must face all of the consequences that this entails. Projects are more concerned for the entire software life-cycle (rather than simply until program implementation), and project management reflects this rather than just the technical aspects of the job.

Above all, software engineers need to work to predetermined standards. These will help to uphold quality, allow easier communication within teams, make it easier for others to continue the work after a change of personnel and, above all, to assist future maintenance tasks. Maintenance is the most arduous and unpopular part of programming. Anything that makes it easier to correct or edit live programs is welcome, even though it appears to deny programmers elements of creativity and originality.

Programs are now generally designed by professionals in standard ways. The design is usually top-down – starting with the overall structure and identifying the order and function of the key modules. Since the resultant design is modular, each module can be worked on separately by team members, some standard modules can be reused from a library of previously coded solutions and modules can be tested in isolation before being tested in combination. Top-down designs also allow the higher-level logic to be expressed independently of machine or language considerations. Programs structured in this way have similarities with each other, leading to greater initial familiarity for newcomers to the project.

The engineering process also applies to standards for testing software, or mathematical proofs of program correctness in terms of the original specification. Testing should be rigorous and thorough, although it cannot, of course, ever prove that a section of code is bug-free.

*see also...*

**Programming language; Software**

79

# Stack

The stack is one of the most important data structures in a computer system. It works in a reverse common sense way, by storing items in the order that they arrive and dealing with them in reverse order. Unlike a queue, which tends to move around in memory (see Data structures), the stack can have a fixed number of locations. The stack pointer is a special register in the central processing unit (CPU) containing the address of the next free location in the stack. It is incremented when a new item is stored (pushed), and decremented when an old item is read from stack (popped). It therefore operates using a principle of last-in first-out.

This is particularly suitable for storing the return address for nested processes. If the CPU is executing a program, and the program calls for a sub-routine to be run, the stack stores the existing program address so that once the sub-routine is complete the CPU can return to where it left off in the main program. The advantage of the stack is that if the sub-routine itself calls another sub-routine then the same thing happens. On exit from the second sub-routine the CPU returns to the first, and on exit from that it returns to the main program. Thus, the return addresses are processed in reverse order. The same principle applies if a process calls itself as a sub-routine (known as recursion), or where one process is interrupted by another.

Another application of stacks is in the evaluation of arithmetic sequences, in what is termed Reverse Polish Notation. When we write arithmetic expressions there is often ambiguity about the order in which operations take place. For example, 'x/y/z' could evaluate to $x/(y \times z)$, or $(x \times z)/y$, depending upon which division occurs first. We try to remove this ambiguity with brackets. The use of brackets is cumbersome, prone to error, and not suitable for computer evaluation. A much simpler system, although strange to us, is to assume that every operation applies to the immediately preceding operands. Thus, 'x+y' would be written 'xy+'. The expression 'xy/z/' is unambiguous since the xy/ has to be evaluated first for there to be two operands for the second division. If such expressions are placed in a stack, they will be removed to be calculated in the correct order.

see also...

Data structure

# Storage device

The main memory storage of a computer generally suffers from one of two important disadvantages. Some is read-only memory (ROM) that, as it name implies, is permanent and not erased by loss of power but whose contents cannot be changed without difficulty. Some is the volatile random-access memory (RAM) where its contents can be altered (written to as well as read from), but are lost or forgotten once the power is switched off. Backing storage devices, such as disc drives, overcome these problems. Data can be written to discs, will remain there in magnetic form without power and can be read back at a later date. The main disadvantage of storage devices is that, like all peripherals, they are much slower than using the main memory. These relative advantages explain why all three types of memory (ROM, RAM and storate devices) are usually present in all systems.

Both tape and disc – the most common forms of storage – operate much more slowly than main memory, but much more quickly than most input/output devices. Tapes are, by their nature, designed to be written to and read from in a predetermined sequence. Tape drives usually have one read/write head which is stationary, while the tape has to travel past the head. They provide only serial access to their contents, but if read serially then they are efficient. Disc drives, on other hand, usually have one read/write head for each usable surface. These heads are on arms that can move in and out from the centre of the disc seeking the appropriate track to read. Tracks are the concentric rings on each surface of the disc where data are stored. Access to the disc therefore has three components. These are the seek time (time taken for the head to move over the right track), the rotational latency (time taken for disc to spin round until required start point in under the head) and the actual time taken to transfer the required data. Serial access such as that provided by tape systems only involves the last of these.

Although there are other forms of storage (optical discs for example), the most common forms are based on tiny areas of local magnetic field created on the iron-oxide coating of the otherwise plastic disc or tape. In time, this coating can disintegrate, causing dropout where data is lost or corrupted.

*see also...*

*Memory; Peripheral*

# Super-Panopticon

The notion of technology as a means of control and power over people has a long tradition, but was perhaps most convincingly explored by the French philosopher Michel Foucault, who traced the development of prisons. Foucault's interest in 'disciplinary technologies' was crystallized in his analysis of Jeremy Bentham's eighteenth-century prison design, the Panopticon. The Panopticon consisted of a series of illuminated cells all facing inwards towards a centrally located observation tower, with windows positioned so as to make it impossible for the prisoner inside a cell to know whether they were actually being observed. The underlying principle was for the prisoner to feel as if they were under inspection at all times. For Foucault, the Panopticon was powerful in that it replaced the crowd by a collection of 'separated individualities', thereby allowing individuals' lives to be 'carefully collated'. The constant knowledge that one is being watched leads to a state of self-policing and the 'automatic functioning of power'.

The rise of IT in society has prompted renewed interest in this particular model of power and control. The surveillance capabilities of new information technologies have been argued to represent a continuation of the disciplinary patterns made explicit in the Panopticon. This can be seen in the computerization of the workplace and the growing use of computerized databases, prompting some commentators to point towards the establishment of 'electronic' and 'information' Panopticons. Most recently, the rise of the Internet and other computerized networks has led commentators to suggest the creation of a 'Super-Panopticon'. This notion of the IT-based Super-Panopticon extends the themes of the Panopticon – surveillance and observation, individualization and totalization, isolation and transparency – through electronic networks.

The account of the Internet as the 'Super-Panopticon' certainly fits in with contemporary concerns over the rise of technological surveillance in society. It is now argued that we live not so much in an information society, as a 'surveillance society', with innumerable electronic networks accumulating information on our everyday activities and transactions.

> ### see also...
> **Internet; Legislation**

# *Syntax*

yntax refers to the rules of grammar in a language, such as a computer programming language. In the same way that it is possible not to understand something said in a natural language because it is not grammatical, so it is possible to write instructions for a computer program that are not valid in the computer language being used. However, unlike natural languages such as English, computers are usually inflexible in understanding anything but the exactly correct form of a programming language. Any deviation from the expected form results in syntax errors that prevent the computer from translating and executing the program. In some cases, mistakes are due to misunderstandings on the part of the programmer, but more usually these are simply typographical errors.

In most languages, the syntax rules are held as a generative grammar, and these rules are neither explicit nor exhaustive. Instead they merely show how valid syntax can be generated. It follows that if these rules cannot generate any specific instruction presented to the translator (assembler, compiler or interpreter), then that instruction must contain a syntax

error. For example, the rules (in a meta-language known as Backus-Naur Form or BNF) for generating a valid whole number for use as an address might be as follows:

```
<number> ::= <sign><digit string>
<sign> ::= '+' | '−' | ''
<digit string> ::= <digit> | <digit><digit string>
<digit>::= '0'|'1' |'2' |'3' |'4' |'5' |'6' |'7' |'8' |'9'
```

In this language, a number consists of an optional sign followed by any sequence of the ten digits. The sequence '-0909' could be generated from the above rules and is therefore grammatically valid, whereas the sequence '2.785' could not (the decimal place is not covered in these rules) and is therefore a syntax error according to the grammar.

When a newly written program is being translated into machine code before execution, any syntax errors will be reported to the programmer via a diagnostic message (such as 'invalid address at line 50'). These errors need to be corrected before the program can be run, since they mean that there is no valid translation and so no machine code equivalent.

## see also...

*Logical error; Programming language; Translation*

# Systems analysis

The term 'systems analysis' is most commonly used in commercial programming environments, where a distinction is drawn between the programmers and the systems analysts who define the parameters of a proposed new system and identify the requirements for that system to meet. This leads to a systems design that is passed to the programmers who implement and test it. Whereas programmers have traditionally been concerned only with designing, coding and testing software, the systems analysts are more concerned with the full system's life-cycle. This cycle goes from idea, to design, to implementation, to testing, to modification, to maintenance, to obsolescence, to new idea (and so on).

However, if a system is taken to be any set of components and their relationship that fulfil a specified task, then the term system analyst takes on a broader meaning. This is actually the original meaning of the term and it might be a useful idea to return to. An organization considering the use of a (new) computer system would hire an analyst. The analyst would look at the existing system, whether manual or automated, and devise an improved one. In many cases, any system in an organization can be improved simply through careful consideration of its original purpose (see Garbage in, garbage out). This may or may not lead to technical change. Technical change alone does not necessarily improve systems. In an extreme case, suppose a manual system was producing the wrong results, then simply automating the current system will only lead to the more efficient production of errors!

Assuming a new system is required, the development stage involves investigation (not simply relying on the executives' version of what they believe goes on in the organization), problem identification and analysis, system design, programming, system testing (as opposed to software testing), documentation and conversion. After implementation would come evaluation, and usually some maintenance. But economic pressure means that in the real world of computing, most systems are actually implemented without complete testing. Documentation and post-live maintenance are therefore vital phases for any system.

*see also...*

*Garbage in, garbage out*

# Technological addiction

As new technologies have risen in prominence, so too have concerns over 'excessive' levels of IT-use amongst certain sections of society, particularly children. Such concerns have led psychologists to view some 'excessive' IT users as suffering from a dependency or addiction to using information technologies, such as computer games and the Internet. To combat these new forms of technology dependency, increasing amounts of time and money are being spent trying to treat such addictions.

As a non-chemical addiction, the definition of technology use as an addictive behaviour draws largely upon the definition of other similar non-chemical addictions such as eating, gambling, sex and exercise. The psychologist Mark Griffiths suggests that technological addiction can be seen to involve six main features:

- *Salience* – when using IT becomes the most important activity in a person's life
- *Mood modification* – when people feel a subjective change in mood (such as a 'high') when using IT
- *Tolerance* – when increasing amounts of IT use are needed to achieve mood modification, initially obtained in less time

- *Withdrawal symptoms* – unpleasant physical effects or feelings when IT use is reduced or discontinued
- *Conflicts* – between using IT and relationships with other people or activities
- *Relapse* – the tendency for extreme IT use to be restored after periods of abstinence or control.

Despite this notion of technological addiction, it remains a complex and contested area of psychology. For example, are users addicted to the physical process of using IT hardware, the interaction with software, the results of using software, or interaction with others via computer mediated communication? Treating 'IT use' as a homogenous activity may make the idea of technological addiction an over-simplification. Thus, many psychologists are beginning to argue that excessive technology usage is often purely symptomatic of wider addictions and only in a minority of cases could the technology be classed as approaching an addiction in itself.

> ### see also...
> Computerphobia; Hackers

# Technological determinism

echnological determinism is the most popular and influential theory of the relationship between technology and society. Put simply, technological determinism is the argument that technology is the principal force that determines the nature of society. Technology is therefore seen as an autonomous force that drives social progress and changes in society in an 'inevitable direction'. Whatever we do, we cannot stop technology having a certain and predetermined effect on our lives.

Although it is rare to find anyone actively claiming to be a technological determinist, the view persists in many contemporary accounts of technology, especially with regards to information technology (IT). Indeed, most popular conceptions of IT are unashamedly based on technological determinism. For example, current perceptions of the Internet's profound and inevitable effects on the way that we work, study and communicate – as well as its 'shrinking' of the world and dissolving of national boundaries – are classic examples of technological determinism.

Such interpretations can appear as 'natural' common sense at first glance and are very appealing to those who wish to speculate on the impact of IT.

Yet, despite its popularity, technological determinism is seen by some people as a dangerous stance to adopt as it ignores the significance of other important forces underlying social change. In fact, many different forces determine the relationship between technology and society. For example, the 'impact' of the Internet could be said to have been as much shaped by the military, big business, politicians and its individual users as by the technology itself.

Approaching IT and society in this one-way 'cause' and 'effect' manner runs the risk of overlooking the many important social, cultural, political and economic forces that also shape both technology and the way we live. Despite this, as an easy and uncomplicated explanation, technological determinism is likely to continue to form the basis of many people's views of the impact of IT on society.

> ### see also...
> Technological utopianism

# Technological fix

The application of technology to the solving of social problems is long established. From the development of the catalytic converter to reduce pollution from car engines to the production of the contraceptive pill to reduce birth rates, technology is often seen as a solution to many of the world's problems. Both of these examples can be seen as 'technological fixes' – attempts to use the power of technology in order to solve problems which are non-technological in nature. Although long-standing, the use of technological fixes in public life has increased immeasurably with the rise of information technologies. Now, for example, information technologies are being heralded as solutions to a variety of social problems – from increasing political participation via Internet-based voting to raising educational standards by using computers in schools. Vast sums of money are being spent around the world to apply IT in a variety of settings with the intention of 'improving' society.

Although social problems are often more complex and harder to solve than technological problems, such technological fixes do sometimes appear to be effective. However, a little more consideration shows that reliance on technology as a ready solution to non-technological problems can be a dangerous stance to adopt. Even if a technology is seen to 'work', it is very difficult to understand why – especially when the application of technology has been accompanied with other non-technological interventions. Technological fixes also tend to produce uneven results – very rarely ending in the same outcomes for all of the population – and often merely replace one social problem with another. Technological fixes can also be criticized for dealing only with the surface manifestations of a problem and not its roots. Indeed, social problems are quantitatively and qualitatively different from technical problems. They tend to be less specific with many different causes and do not operate within a closed system like many technological problems. The roots of social problems are social in nature and therefore ultimately require social solutions. This of course, is a far more difficult, timely, expensive and often imprecise course of action – hence the enduring attraction of the comparatively instant technological fix.

*see also...*

**Technological determinism**

# *Technological utopianism*

**D**eriving from the Greek words for not (*ou*) and place (*topos*), the concept of 'utopia' was first coined by Sir Thomas More at the beginning of the sixteenth century to denote an ideal city-state whose citizens lived under apparently perfect conditions. The term 'utopianism' has come to refer to idealistic visions of a perfect world that are unachievable in practice. Since More, many authors have written from a utopian viewpoint – speculating on a range of social possibilities set in the near-future. As a genre of writing, utopianism serves to stimulate hope regarding the future, as well as acting as a stimulus for action to achieve such hopes in practice.

From its origins in political and social satire, utopianism has, in recent times, become an especially prominent feature of popular accounts of IT and society. Indeed, technological utopianism pervades many accounts of IT and of the potential effects it may have on society. Optimistic and often exaggerated stories are prominent with regard to the beneficial effects of technologies such as the Internet in the areas of education, business, leisure and government. Visions of the Internet leading to democratic and unconstrained 'virtual communities' are clear examples of technological utopianism – describing alternative IT-based worlds where existing social problems are ameliorated and overcome via the development of technology. These stories all conform to the pattern of a new technology playing a crucial role in creating a utopian society or way of life – where the vast majority of individual users are effortlessly empowered and liberated in ways hitherto impossible.

Technological utopian accounts of IT and society can be criticized as being overtly determinist in their approach, seeing technology as the primary driving force in creating these 'better' societies. Furthermore, the force and conviction with which such accounts are often presented to the general public almost always leads to a cycle of misleading expectations and eventual disappointment when these expectations are not fulfilled. Technological utopianism could be an unhealthy perspective to adapt, but it is one that persists in society as 'new' technologies are developed at a faster rate than 'older' technologies that are seen to fail to fulfil their promise.

*see also...*

*Futurology; Luddism*

# Technology

Deriving from the Greek word for craft or skill (*techne*), the term technology was not coined until the 1820s. At its broadest level, technology can be seen as the development of tools and techniques to control nature and overcome natural human limitations. In this respect, technology is a vital aspect of human survival. Humans are physiologically limited as a species, but have an ability to develop and apply technology to overcome these limitations. In this way, technology can help humans do things that they could not do before (such as communicating with people around the world) or do things far more easily, quickly and cheaply (such as writing a book using a word processor).

Yet to see technology merely in terms of artefacts or hardware and the associated ways of using them is to overlook the 'human' aspects of technology that are just as important. In other words, technology is not just a matter of tools and techniques. Indeed, the development and application of technologies does not take place in a vacuum. The development, production and application of even the simplest technology requires the efforts and skills of many different people. When you sit down to use a computer you are doing

so through a complex organization of people and firms who have got you to that point. The basis of any technology is a host of artefacts, skills and organizations. It is therefore easier to conceptualize it in terms of being a system of technical and social components coming together. Seeing technology as a system consisting of technical, organizational, social, economic and even political factors allows us to understand the often complex and messy nature of technological change. Thus, as the sociologist Rudi Volti suggests, we can perhaps best see technology as 'a system based on the application of knowledge, manifested in physical objects and organizational forms, for the attainment of specific goals'.

## see also...

*Information and communications technology*

# Teleworking

Teleworking (or telecommuting) refers to a situation where people work outside of their principal place of employment via electronic connections. Such off-site working is most popularly seen to take place at home, leading many people to argue that information technologies such as the fax, Internet and video-conferencing are set to radically alter the conventional patterns of working life. The perceived benefits of this are plenty. For the employer, teleworking reduces the costs of overheads, time lost to commuting and is argued to improve employee productivity, as well as being a major factor in attracting and retaining staff. For the employee, teleworking is seen to offer flexibility, reduced levels of stress, as well as increased motivation and satisfaction. Finally, at a societal level, teleworking is seen to open up employment opportunities for social groups previously limited by issues of time and mobility – such as mothers, the disabled and older workers – as well as reducing levels of traffic congestion and pollution.

In theory, teleworking is a good example of how the application of IT can have a positive impact on our lives. However, teleworking is not a universal panacea to employment and work-related problems.

Technically, teleworking can be used only in areas of employment that are primarily paper or communication based. Jobs that involve the production of goods by the manipulation of materials or dealing with the public are obviously less suited to teleworking. Steelworkers, for example, are unlikely to find themselves teleworking in the near future. Moreover, at an organizational level, teleworking alters the levels and nature of communication within a firm and, therefore, the nature of the organization itself.

Teleworking is a good example of the advantages and disadvantages of 'remote' applications of ICT. Of course, work and employment are social activities as well as merely involving the delivery of information, but it is the former aspects that are missing in all forms of teleworking. Teleworking may well overcome some logistical problems, but also runs the risk of introducing different social ones at the same time.

## see also...

Information society

# Time–space compression

Time–space compression is a geographical term referring to the apparent contraction of geographic space and distance by transport and communication technologies. It is a way of describing how space and the distance between people and places have become less important as barriers as technologies have developed. A striking example of time–space compression is the way that our spatial sense of the Atlantic Ocean changed with the invention of the jet aircraft. Suddenly, a journey from London to New York could be achieved in hours rather than weeks, thus diminishing the 'friction' of transatlantic distance. For many commentators, a 'new round' of time–space compression has occurred with the emergence of global telecommunications and information technologies such as the Internet. Here, the tremendous speed that information can be transported around the world has, in some eyes, led to a total collapse of time and distance. Via the Internet, it is claimed that you can communicate or do business with any other Internet user, regardless of physical or temporal proximity – 'anytime, anyplace, anywhere'.

Of course, this is a hugely generalized view. Above all, it is crucial to remember that time–space compression is not uniform. Just as the development of the helicopter has only altered the time–space compression of travelling from city to city for a minority of people, the Internet has only facilitated such changes for those who have access to it. Telecommunications technologies have made little difference in terms of time–space compression of sub-Saharan Africa for the vast majority of people who live there. Similarly, telecommunications technologies (akin to cars, trains and other transport technologies) run on many different routes that vary in capacity and speed. Therefore, time–space compression is uneven over different spaces, with different people having different levels of access to fast telecommunications.

Despite such caveats, the compression of time and space by IT is of considerable economic and political importance. Furthermore, for the more philosophically inclined, the disconnection of places and time is seen as being at the root of the 'post-modern condition', where people's sense of self, belonging and place in the world are no longer as fixed and rigid as they once were.

## see also...
*Global village*

# Translation

Computer processors can execute only a relatively small range of simple instructions that are known collectively as the processor's 'machine code'. Each type of processor has a different machine code, and therefore programs written for one type (or make) of computer can not be executed successfully on any other. Technically, machine code is not 'portable' between machines. Partly because of this, and partly because it is not easy for humans to work with binary machine code, programs are usually written in some other format (a programming language) and then translated into machine code before execution.

The translation process is carried out by another program (usually called an assembler, compiler, interpreter, or program generator) which converts the source code (in which the program is written) into object (or machine) code. The translation program is designed to convert source code into a specified machine code. Therefore, like the machine code itself, it is not portable. However, the source code *can* be written in a programming language which is capable of being translated into different machine codes. Source code is therefore usually portable, and the same program can be translated to run on different machines.

Each instruction in machine code consists of a simple operation (binary codes representing Add or Move) and one or more operands (binary numbers representing machine addresses or literal values). A symbolic version of such a machine code is known as assembly code. This allows the programmer to write the program using mnemonic, or easy to remember, instructions (such as ADD rather than a binary code) and symbolic addresses or variables (such as TOTAL instead of a binary address). High-level programming languages, such as Pascal or COBOL, are even easier to use and less machine-orientated than assembly code.

Before execution, a program written in a programming language, such as assembly code, needs to be translated into machine code. The translation can then be stored in object form, and executed as many times as needed without re-translation. The translation program converts the symbolic instructions into machine code and the variables and data structures into machine addresses.

> **see also...**
>
> *Execution cycle; Programming language; Syntax*

# Turing, Alan

Alan Turing (1912–54) was a British mathematician who developed many of the theoretical foundations for modern-day digital computing. At the beginning of the 1930s, Turing began to concentrate on the question of 'Decidability', known in mathematical circles as the Entscheidungsproblem, that questioned whether there was a process that could ascertain whether any mathematical problem was provable or not. Unlike other mathematicians working on the Entscheidungsproblem at the time, Turing was interested in the solving of mathematical problems through mechanical means.

In 1936, Turing published a paper in which he proposed an abstract model for a logical machine that could calculate any mathematical problem. This general model quickly became known as the 'Turing Machine' and pre-empted the design and development of some aspects of the digital computer. The Turing Machine was conceived as three main elements: a long tape that was divided into squares that could either be left blank or contain a symbol; a scanner which could scan each square on the tape individually and either read, write or erase its contents; and finally, a set (or program) of instructions. In his paper, Turing demonstrated how any calculation could be achieved by including the instructions in a standard form on the tape, thus making the Turing Machine capable of many different operations. Although it would take nine years before the electronic technology would be developed to allow Turing to put his ideas into practice, this abstract concept of the Turing Machine provided the essential characteristic of the modern-day computer – a machine that can be applied to any well-defined task given an appropriate set of instructions.

During World War II, Turing became well known for overseeing the construction of the deciphering machine tackling the Enigma code. After the war, he worked towards the construction of a machine that would put his Turing Machine principles into action – the Automatic Computing Engine. In 1951, Turing wrote another seminal paper in which he explored the potential for thinking machines, proposing the 'Turing Test' for artificial intelligence that is still used to this day.

*see also...*

**Artificial intelligence; Computer**

# Universal access

Universal access is one of the most important technological issues facing governments in the information age. Although definitions of universal access vary, it can be seen broadly as the desire to make information technology available to *all* citizens. In other words, to ensure that all citizens should have the opportunity to use IT at an affordable cost. Achieving universal access to technology is seen to be important as IT is used more and more for the delivery of public and commercial services. This has led some governments to argue that universal access is a basic right for full participation in a modern democratic society – avoiding the problems associated with the 'digital divide'.

Yet, in practice, universal access is not easily achievable. Even apparently ubiquitous technologies such as the television and telephone are not universal. In the UK and USA, for example, just over 90 per cent of the population have access to a telephone – leaving a substantial minority without. Thus, governments tend to talk of universal access, but actually mean ensuring that 'the majority' or 'most' citizens have access to IT. One popular strategy to help provide access to technology for those who cannot afford it, has been to make technology publicly available. This can be seen in governments' attempts to make Internet access available in libraries, museums, community centres and other public places, along with offering subsidized basic IT skills training. In theory, therefore, even if you do not own a computer, you can still gain access to the Internet.

One of the principal problems with universal access is the definition of 'access'. Although having physical access to technology is important, it is meaningless without the requisite skills to use it and the ability to then access the information and services. Access to IT does not ensure use. Therefore, governments cannot ensure that all citizens make use of IT – they can only provide the opportunity for use. Secondly, beyond the simple issue of 'access/no access' to IT come more complex questions of levels of connectivity in terms of the capability and distribution of the access concerned. These caveats point to the enduring nature of social inequalities despite ever-rising levels of IT use in society.

**see also...**

*Digital divide*

94

# Verification and validation

**V**erification and validation refer to the array of checks built into a computer system to detect and prevent errors in the system. Verification and validation reduce the likelihood that computer systems are working with corrupt data. This is vital since, although results from computers are often assumed to be automatically correct, it remains the case that a computer application based on incorrect information produces incorrect results (Garbage in, garbage out).

The term verification describes checks for errors in which the requirement for 'good' data is very strict. For example, when changing their security password a user is often required to enter their new password twice. Only when precisely the same data has been entered twice is the password updated. This is a form of verification that prevents the user from changing the password inadvertently. Similar approaches are used within computer systems to check that data has been transmitted correctly between different components (i.e. by sending the message twice and comparing the two received versions for differences).

Validation describes checks for errors in which the requirement for 'good' data is plausibility. For example, when entering new data to a payroll system a validity check might reject a negative value for the number of hours worked. In software design, many validity checks are 'range checks', only allowing processing to continue if the values involved are all within an expected range. Validation is also used to check that data from a storage device has not been corrupted during storage, and that the correct file is being used for a particular process.

It is this idea of validation that provided the basis for the fears about the 'Millennium Bug' during the changeover from 1999 to 2000. The original, and very rational, fear was that software had been designed in the twentieth century with validation routines based on years with two digits (such as 87 or 93) and may have also been programmed to reject digits lower than the year of software design (such as 00). If this were the case, the software would not run until it was re-engineered. This technical concern then led to more general fears that many computers would 'crash' on New Year's Eve 1999, including household appliances that used no date function at all!

## see also...

*Data; Garbage in, garbage out*

# Virtual community

The term 'virtual community' was popularized by the Californian writer Howard Rheingold, who defined it as 'the social aggregations that emerge from the Internet when enough people carry on those public discussions long enough, with sufficient human feeling, to form webs of personal relationships in cyberspace.' Examples of virtual communities can be found all over the Internet in the form of on-line chatrooms, news groups, e-mail bulletin boards and multi-user role playing sites. Indeed, Rheingold's initial descriptions of virtual communities were based on his experience of the Whole Earth 'Lectronic Link (WELL), an early e-mail-based 'community'.

The notion of virtual community builds upon the long-held enthusiasm amongst technologists for computer mediated communication and its potential for altering and creating new forms of social relations. In particular, it is based upon the ideal of the Internet being a democratic tool – allowing each user an equal right to speak with others regardless of proximity and shared physical experience. The idea, then, that groups of individuals from all over the world can get together on-line and interact with each other in virtual communities has given rise to the argument that such gatherings have the potential to improve upon, or even replace, real-life face-to-face interactions. From this perspective, on-line communication is seen as a powerful means for specialist, but disparate, groups of like-minded individuals to form democratic virtual communities, providing mutual support, advice and identity.

Of course, such utopian views of computer mediated communication leading to a reinvention of 'community' ignores the mundane reality of many such on-line groups. Many critics argue that on-line communities should not be classed as such since they are self-selecting and transient; lacking the crucial element of a common obligation between members and therefore devaluing the nature of any 'community' debate or action. As the Internet academic Steven Jones concludes, 'the Internet allows us to shout more loudly, but whether our fellows listen is questionable, and whether our words make a difference is even more in doubt'.

## see also...

Computer mediated communication

# *Virtual machine*

A virtual machine is a simple-to-use imaginary computer that the operating system presents as a facade to the user. The operating system deals with the complexities of internal codes, interrupts, memory management, peripheral transfers, scheduling and other 'housekeeping' activities. This leaves the user free to deal with the simpler, but often more important, tasks. This is generally so successful that most users are unaware that the 'machine' they are interacting with is a very simplified version of the actual hardware. This is particularly the case with Macintosh PCs, for example, where the user is even isolated from the appearance of the operating system by the construction of a virtual desktop and pseudo-physical objects (representing both hardware and software items) that can be moved around on screen. Although there are significant differences between different computers in terms of their circuitry, memory design and so on, they are all based around the same basic 'central processing unit with peripherals' design. It is their respective operating systems that make computers appear more different than they are by creating different styles of virtual machine.

Virtual memory is memory space in the central processing unit (CPU) which is available to the user but that does not actually exist. A program and its associated graphics and data may require more memory space than is available at any time, but by using virtual memory this shortage does not prevent the program from running. A portion of the program is loaded into main memory, and the remainder is held on backing storage. As the program executes, it will be necessary for the operating system to load further sections of program and data into memory, over-writing what is already there.

The term 'virtual' is now in common usage, appearing in phrases such as virtual screen and virtual reality. In each example, it means the same thing – the construction through software of a 'real' object or process. A virtual screen is similar to the use of multiple 'windows' on one actual screen. The actual screen is the hardware monitor, but the display can give the appearance of many screens, either one behind the other, or one within another.

> *see also...*
>
> **Memory; Operating system**

# Virtual reality

**V**irtual reality (VR) refers to the use of computer hardware and software to create the effect of three-dimensional environments which users can move through and interact with. Crucially, such environments create the effect of objects having a 3D spatial presence, independent of both the user and the computer technology. On a popular level, VR has often been extended to include any form of virtual world represented by a computer – even at the level of text-based environments such as role playing games. However, whereas these latter applications require the user to imagine a virtual world, virtual reality technology is distinct in actually creating such environments through human senses, such as sight, sound and touch.

At the moment, the hype and excitement surrounding virtual reality has been tempered by the unwieldy hardware needed to sustain such environments. Users have to wear special headsets, gloves and bodysuits that are connected to a computer system; feeding sensory input to the user through sound, sight and touch as well as reacting to the user's actions.

However, it is the social and psychological effects rather than technological practicalities that make virtual reality an important area of IT development. Enthusiasts argue that VR will have profound implications for the way in which we communicate and interact with others, with people no longer constricted by distance, time or physical attributes like location or body. In this way, users will be able to construct different 'virtual identities' and virtual bodies through which they can experience these 'virtual' worlds. The key advantage being that users have control over both their environment and themselves.

Virtual reality introduces a host of questions concerning the changing values of reality and simulation in a technology-based society. Indeed, from a more theoretical perspective, VR blurs the boundaries between what is real-life 'reality' and 'virtual reality'. Such concerns have been explored by the French philosopher Jean Baudrillard who points to the emergence of 'Hyperreality'; a condition whereby models and simulations replace 'the real' and eventually become much more authentic objects in our lives than the original itself.

> ### see also...
> *Cyberpunk; Interactivity*

# Virus

A virus is a piece of program code that is loaded onto a computer without its user's knowledge and then goes on to perform detrimental or destructive functions, ranging from displaying unwanted messages through to destroying data and preventing the user from accessing information (referred to as denial of service). The simplest version of this, known as a Trojan Horse, is a virus masquerading as a useful program (such as a game or even a virus protection application) that when downloaded onto a computer goes on to have detrimental effects. This principle also underlies the current trend for e-mail viruses where a virus is attached to a seemingly benign e-mail message (such as the 'I love you' virus) and is only executed when users open the message. More sophisticated variants include 'worms', that are programs capable of replicating themselves over a computer network from computer to computer and then using up computer time and slowing networks down – sometimes to the point of shutting systems down completely. It is this destructive and often malicious nature of viruses that make them so feared by most computer users.

Like biological viruses, computer viruses are passed from computer to computer through some form of contact – usually on the back of another program or document. They are able to spread quickly due to the connectivity of computers and the increased sharing and transferring of software and code by computer users across networks. So much data is now transferred over the Internet that viruses have increased in their ability to spread on a global basis – as seen in recent world scares over viruses such as the Code Red worm that was designed to slow down Internet servers and specifically to bombard the White House Internet server with spurious requests for data and therefore cause it to cease operation.

Unlike biological viruses, computer viruses are completely man-made and are usually the work of disaffected or mischievous programmers. Whereas some programmers create a virus for purely destructive purposes, others see it as a technical challenge or a high profile means of competing with their peers. Some programmers, known as crackers, seek to create viruses to demonstrate weaknesses in computer security for large firms or government agencies.

## see also...

**Hackers; Legislation**

# von Neumann, John

John von Neumann (1903–57) was a Hungarian–American mathematician who, after studying science and mathematics throughout his childhood and adolescence, moved to Princeton University at the beginning of the 1930s, just as his academic counterparts began to become interested in computing machines. However, whereas most academic mathematicians were concerning themselves with developing machines to calculate tables, von Neumann saw the possibility of applying computing machines to a range of specific mathematical problems. This eventually led von Neumann to develop the architectural structure for a computer that remains the basis for the design of computers today – known as the von Neumann machine.

Von Neumann developed a model for a stored program computer, where the set of instructions (the program) and the data that the instructions refer to, are kept together in the computer's memory. The computer also consists of a control unit and arithmetic-logic unit that determine which actions will be carried out by sequentially reading the instructions from the program stored in the memory. Finally, input and output devices allow the computer to be programmed and the results of its calculations to be displayed. This is the form of most modern computers.

Despite his pioneering work, von Neumann's work with computers received relatively little attention at the time of his death, with obituary writers preferring to concentrate on his numerous other achievements in mathematics, game theory, nuclear weaponry and quantum mechanics. Now his work on computers is so established that any computer not conforming to his model is specifically referred to as having 'non von Neumann architecture'.

## see also...

Central processing unit; Computer

# World wide web

Throughout the 1970s and 1980s, the Internet was a relatively unwieldy environment for anyone other than the scientists and academics who were regularly using it. However, this all changed with the development of the world wide web; a global hypertext space of information based around the Internet.

The world wide web – also abbreviated as 'the web', www or W3 – was originally developed by a team of physicists, led by Tim Berners-Lee. Their intention was to extend the usefulness of the Internet by developing 'hypertext' links between different documents available on the Internet. This would allow the user to follow pathways of interest by clicking on words or links within documents that would then jump to another part of the document or even a related document on another server system. This ambition was realized by the team's development of a new Internet protocol called 'hypertext transfer protocol' (HTTP) and an associated language called 'hypertext mark-up language' (HTML) that supported links to other documents. Each page of information was given its own unique address known as a Universal Resource Locator (URL) acting as a signpost and allowing users to jump from one location on the web to another.

In its infancy, the world wide web remained unwieldy to use until the development of graphical interfaces – known as web browsers – which allowed users to interact with the web by simply pointing a screen-based cursor at links and clicking. It was the development of web browsers that opened up the world wide web and the Internet to a mass, general audience who no longer needed a knowledge of complex programming languages and protocols. The development of software to search through all the pages of information available on the web and look for key words or attributes (known as search engines) further extended the usefulness of the world wide web for the general user. The web opened the Internet up to a general audience because it overcame the need for technical knowledge. Its subsequent popularity is testament to the web's ease of use and networked architecture that allows users to browse (or 'surf') many different sources of information.

### see also...

*Cyberspace; E-mail, Hypertext; Internet*

# Further Reading

There are many reference books giving further details of the technical aspects of IT. The following texts provide more detailed discussion of the more socially orientated key ideas highlighted in this book.

Asimov, Issac (1971) *I, Robot*, London: Collins

Baudrillard, Jean (1983) *Simulations*, New York: Semiotext

Bell, David and Barbara Kennedy (ed.) (2000) *The Cybercultures Reader*, London: Routledge

Castells, Manuel (2000) *The Information Age: Economy, Society and Culture (three Volumes)* 2nd Edition, Oxford: Blackwell

Dutton, William (ed.) (1996) *Information and Communication Technologies: Visions and Realities*, Oxford: Oxford University Press

Foucault, Michel (1975) *Discipline and Punish*, London: Penguin

Griffiths, Mark (1995) 'Technological Addictions' from *Clinical Psychology Forum*, Vol. 76, pp.14–19

Hawisher, Gail and Cynthia Selfe (ed.) (1997) *Literacy, Technology and Society: Confronting the Issues,* New York: Prentice Hall

Jones, Steven (ed.) (1998) *Cybersociety 2.0*, London: Sage

Lovelace, Ada (1843) 'Sketch of the Analytical Engine by L.F. Menabrea' from *Taylor's Scientific Memoirs*, Vol. 3, pp. 689–90

Levinson, Paul (1997) *The Soft Edge: a Natural History and Future of the Information Revolution*, London: Routledge

Luehrmann, Arthur (1981) 'Computer Literacy – What Should It Be?' from *The Mathematics Teacher*, Vol. 74 no. 9, pp. 682–686

Mayer, Paul (ed.) (1999) *Computer Media and Communication: a Reader*, Oxford: Oxford University Press

Negroponte, Nicholas (1995) *Being Digital*, London: Coronet

Nelson, Ted (1980) *Literary Machines*, Sausalito, CA: Minefield Press

Rheingold, Howard (1994) *The Virtual Community*, London: Secker & Warburg

Selwyn, Neil and Stephen Gorard (2002) *The Information Age,* Cardiff: University of Wales Press

Teich, Albert (ed.) (1999) *Technology and the Future (Eighth Edition)*, New York: St. Martin's Press

Volti, Rudi (1992) *Society and Technological Change (Second Edition)*, New York: St. Martins Press

Wise, Richard (2000) *Multimedia: a Critical Introduction*, London: Routledge

# *Also available in the series*

| | | |
|---|---|---|
| **TY 101 Key Ideas: Astronomy** | Jim Breithaupt | 0 340 78214 5 |
| **TY 101 Key Ideas: Buddhism** | Mel Thompson | 0 340 78028 2 |
| **TY 101 Key Ideas: Business Studies** | Neil Denby | 0 340 80435 1 |
| **TY 101 Key Ideas: Chemistry** | Andrew Scott | 0 340 80392 4 |
| **TY 101 Key Ideas: Ecology** | Paul Mitchell | 0 340 78209 9 |
| **TY 101 Key Ideas: Economics** | Keith Brunskill | 0 340 80436 X |
| **TY 101 Key Ideas: Evolution** | Morton Jenkins | 0 340 78210 2 |
| **TY 101 Key Ideas: Existentialism** | George Myerson | 0 340 78152 1 |
| **TY 101 Key Ideas: Genetics** | Morton Jenkins | 0 340 78211 0 |
| **TY 101 Key Ideas: Linguistics** | Richard Horsey | 0 340 78213 7 |
| **TY 101 Key Ideas: Philosophy** | Paul Oliver | 0 340 78029 0 |
| **TY 101 Key Ideas: Physics** | Jim Breithaupt | 0 340 79048 2 |
| **TY 101 Key Ideas: Politics** | Peter Joyce | 0 340 79961 7 |
| **TY 101 Key Ideas: Psychology** | Dave Robinson | 0 340 78155 6 |
| **TY 101 Key Ideas: World Religions** | Paul Oliver | 0 340 79049 0 |